ACHIEVING
EYPS

Childhood Observation

ACHIEVING
EYPS

Childhood Observation

Ioanna Palaiologou

Series editors: Gill Goodliff and Lyn Trodd

LearningMatters

First published in 2008 by Learning Matters Ltd
Reprinted in 2009

British Library Cataloguing in Publication Data
A CIP record for this book is available from the British Library

ISBN 978 1 84445 173 9

Cover design by Phil Barker
Text design by Code 5 Design Associates Ltd
Project Management by Swales & Willis Ltd, Exeter, Devon
Typeset by Kelly Gray
Printed and bound by TJ International Ltd, Padstow, Cornwall

Learning Matters
33 Southernhay East
Exeter EX1 1NX
Tel: 01392 215560
info@learningmatters.co.uk
www.learningmatters.co.uk

Dedication

To George for the nice memories.

Contents

Foreword from the series editors

This book is one of a series which will be of interest to all those following pathways towards achieving Early Years Professional Status (EYPS). This includes students on Sector-Endorsed Foundation Degree in Early Years programmes and undergraduate Early Childhood Studies degree courses as these awards are key routes towards EYPS.

The graduate EYP role was developed as a key strategy in government commitment to improve the quality of Early Years care and education in England, especially in the private, voluntary and independent sectors. Policy documents and legislation such as *Every Child Matters: Change for Children* DfES (2004); the *Ten Year Childcare Strategy: Choice for Parents – the Best Start for Children* HMT (2004), and the Childcare Act, 2006, identified the need for high-quality, well-trained and educated professionals to work with the youngest children. At the time of writing (July 2008), the Government's aim is to have Early Years Professionals (EYPs) in all Children's Centres by 2010 and in every full day care setting by 2015.

In *Childhood Observation* Ioanna Palaiologou draws on her experience of teaching Early Years practitioners to provide a book that contextualises the required knowledge and understanding of the EYP role in relation to observation, assessment and recording. The book makes links to the National Standards for Early Years Professional Status and to the principles of the Early Years Foundation Stage. Case studies, reflective and practical tasks are used to deepen readers' understanding and skill development.

This book is distinctive in the series because it provides essential underpinning knowledge for effective practice required by candidates who wish to achieve EYP Status. It aims to deepen the understanding of its readers so that they become more aware of why and how young children's learning and development is supported through observation. The purpose of each chapter is to give EYPs the tools they need to reflect on their own practice in observing children and the skills to lead and influence other practitioners.

Childhood Observation will support candidates on any of the pathways towards achieving Early Years Professional Status and we are delighted to commend it to you.

Gill Goodliff
The Open University

Lyn Trodd
University of Hertfordshire
July 2008

About the author and series editors

Ioanna Palaiologou

Ioanna Palaiologou originally qualified as an Early Years teacher. She studied for her Masters degree in Educational Psychology and then completed her PhD at Nottingham University investigating young children's responses to a cognitive-oriented intervention programme. Ioanna worked at the University of Wales Swansea as a Lecturer on Early Childhood Studies degree courses and the University of Hull as Programme Director of the BA (Hons) Educational Studies. Ioanna is currently working as a Senior Lecturer and researcher at Nottingham Trent University, contributing modules at the BA (Honours) Childhood Studies degree.

Gill Goodliff

Gill Goodliff is a Lecturer in Early Years at the Open University where she teaches on work-based learning courses in the Sector-Endorsed Foundation Degree in Early Years and is a Lead Assessor for Early Years Professional Status. Her professional background with young children and their families was predominantly in the Public Voluntary and Independent sector. Her current research focuses on the professional development and identities of Early Years practitioners and young children's spirituality.

Lyn Trodd

Lyn Trodd is a Principal Lecturer and Head of Children's Workforce Development at the University of Hertfordshire. She is currently Chair of the Sector-Endorsed Foundation Degree in Early Years national network. Lyn was a member of the Children's Workforce Development Council reference group consulted about the new status for Early Years Professionals and led a team which piloted EYPS at the University of Hertfordshire. Her research is focused on graduate roles for members of the Children Workforce and how professional learning programmes develop self-efficacy in participants.

Introduction

Introduction

The field of Early Years care and education has seen radical changes in the past decade. A large number of policies, reforms, initiatives and Acts have been introduced with the aim of improving quality in Early Years, and to increase the standards of Early Years care and education. The implementation of the Every Child Matters green paper (DfES, 2003) and the subsequent Children Act of 2004 brought about changes within the Early Years. The introduction of a national framework – The Early Years Foundation Stage – as implemented from September 2008. Similarly, the workforce in the Early Years has seen changes, aimed at raising quality and training among people working in the sector.

The introduction of the Early Years Professional Status (a 'status', not 'qualification') will be seen as the 'gold standard' (HM Government, 2006a) which will raise standards in Early Years workforce training, in an attempt to meet the quality requirements of the EYFS. The Common Assessment Framework (CAF) – a multi professional approach to integrate services across the children's and young people's sector – was implemented in April 2006. The Common Assessment Framework was developed with the intention of understanding children's needs at an earlier stage so that joined up support can be offered to children, bringing together families alongside the Early Years workforce and other agencies, such as the social services and health visitors.

The aim of this introductory chapter is to consider the current key policy drivers and to highlight the role of observation and assessments within this changing context.

Before you read any further, reflect on your own experiences of Early Years education. Think back to your own childhood. Can you remember what Early Years provision you experienced? If so what do you remember about these experiences?

Think about the following.

1 The physical environment and the types of activities that you were involved in.

2 How many other children were there?

3 What do you think you gained from attending an Early Years setting – what were the adults trying to achieve with you?

Policy context

The United Nations Convention on the Rights of the Child, (UNCRC) adopted by the United Nations General Assembly in 1989, brought about changes in terms of policy making and their implementation for children. The UNCRC is an agreement between the United Nations and the individual countries belonging to the United Nations that have chosen to ratify the Convention. Central to the Convention is the recognition that all children have the right to education. It stated that all children should have access to free education and the UN nations involved are responsible to provide this. It also recognises diversity among children and the issue of equal opportunities, no matter the socio-economic, political or racial group to which each child belongs.

Countries that have ratified the UNCRC have a commitment to deliver the rights of the child and to incorporate and apply these rights to their policies for children. The Convention has had great impact on services and policies for children at a national and international level.

The UK ratified the Convention on16 December 1991, and it came into force from 15 January 1992.

New Labour policy focuses on minimising poverty and increasing the quality of care and education of children, along with the recommendations of the Laming Inquiry, following the death of Victoria Climbié (see http://www.victoria-climbie-inquiry.org.uk/). This led to the *Every Child Matters* (DfES, 2003) green paper and the subsequent Children Act of 2004.

Within *Every Child Matters* (ECM), it is expected that a number of services will work together to meet the five outcomes.

✓ Be healthy

✓ Be safe

✓ Enjoy and achieve

✓ To make a positive contribution

✓ To achieve economic well-being

Central to the *Every Child Matters* and *Youth Matters* papers is the protection of children and the prevention of things from going wrong. The Common Assessment Framework, the notion of the 'lead professional', and the sharing of information have all been developed in an attempt to become useful tools within the children's workforce for meeting the outcomes of Every Child Matters.

Multi agency working with children and families is key to high quality and effective Early Years practice. The Common Assessment Framework is aimed to be the result of multi-agency work. A number of different services are asked to communicate with regards to identifying additional children's needs not covered by any other service at an early stage, and to provide support and intervention for children and their families. The Common Assessment Framework for children and young people is one of the elements in the delivery of integrated frontline services. It is aimed to share assessment information about a child across all children's services and local authority areas, in an attempt to identify early on any needs that a child might have, and to try to ensure that these needs are met. It consists of the following.

- A shared process to enable practitioners to undertake a common assessment and then act on the result.

- A standard form to record the assessment.

- A pre-assessment checklist to help decide who would benefit from a common assessment.

It is expected that people in the children's workforce should understand the ECM outcomes, have knowledge of the CAF, and be able to effectively complete a CAF checklist. Individual organisations offering services for children are responsible for having at least one member of staff trained to be able to meet the CAF requirements and procedures.

Under the CAF there are four main procedures.

- Check whether there is already an assessment for a child, and if not then prepare to undertake one.

- Carry out an assessment.

- Identify the appropriate support – for example, liaising with other services to plan a common approach to address problems.

- Ask parents to participate with the assessment when any concerns are raised.

Important aspects of the implementation of the CAF are as follows.

- Gathering information: an important tool in gathering information is observation, especially when young children are involved. There are pre-set assessment checklists available for practitioners to use. These checklists are mostly related to children's development.

- Sharing information: once an assessment has taken place the records should be kept safe and confidential, and yet also accessible, in order to enable children and families to address their needs in an appropriate way and with the appropriate services.

- The role of the lead professional is to ensure that information is gathered, to liaise with all relevant services, and to plan any appropriate action if it is required. Fundamental skills for the lead professional are the ability to understand systematic observations, and to record and share findings.

The Government intends to move towards integrated services, whereby a number of professionals from different areas are working together for effective practice with children. On 1 October 2006 the Children's Workforce Development Council (CWDC) became responsible for the implementation of the CAF. Among its duties was to ensure that the workforce of the children's services were acquiring common skills and knowledge, as the goal is to bring all professionals from different sectors to work together in order to meet the five outcomes of the ECM.

The CWDC vision is of a workforce that:

- supports integrated and coherent services for children, young people and families;

- remains stable and appropriately staffed, whilst exhibiting flexibility and responsiveness;

- is trusted and accountable, and thereby valued;

- demonstrates a high level of skills, productivity and effectiveness;

- exhibits strong leadership, management and supervision.

(http://www.cwdcouncil.org.uk/projects/earlyyears.htm)

As a result, the CWDC sets out a Common Core of Skills and Knowledge for the Children's Workforce. The common core skills are the basic levels of skills and knowledge that all people working with children should meet. This set of skills and knowledge is organised under six headings.

- Effective communication and engagement with children, young people and families.

- Child and young person development (this covers aspects of child development).

- Safeguarding and promoting the welfare of the child.

- Supporting transitions (i.e. supporting children through either developmental or environmental changes, and supporting children in their given context).

- Multi-agency working.

- Sharing information.

The new children's workforce will be able to work in the following settings.

- Children's Centres (multi agency providers of services for children and families);

- Early Excellence centres (models of integrated services);

- extended schools;

- Foundation Stage units;
- integrated centres (local facilities to provide integrated early child care and education);
- nurseries;
- neighbourhood nurseries;
- Sure Start local programmes.

In all Ofsted registered settings where there are children from 0–5 the Early Years Foundation Stage as implemented from September 2008 is statutory.

PRACTICAL TASK

From your own experience can you identify the advantages and disadvantages of multi-agency work for children?

In your discussion consider the following.

1 Lack of knowledge of services

2 Poverty

3 Cultural factors

The Early Years Foundation Stage

In the field of Early Years the introduction and implementation of the Early Years Foundation Stage (EYFS) as a single quality framework becomes a reality in September 2008. The quality framework was determined by three different documents: the *Curriculum Guidance for the Foundation Stage*, the *Birth to Three Matters* framework and the *National Standards for Under 8s Daycare and Childminding* (DfES, 2007). The EYFS brings these three documents together into one cohesive framework. The overall aim of the EYFS is to incorporate the five outcomes of the ECM (DfES, 2007).

The EYFS aims to become an integrated approach to care and education for children, from birth to the end of the Foundation Stage. It emphasises the importance of play and it attempts to help practitioners to plan care and learning that is appropriate for each child at each stage of their development. It also emphasises outdoor play and asks the providers to revisit their practices in terms of outdoors activities, and to encourage outdoor play on a daily basis (DCSF, 2008a).

It also aims to:

✓ strengthen the links between Birth to Three Matters and the Foundation Stage;

✓ incorporate elements of the National Standards;

✓ ensure a consistent approach to care, learning and development from birth to the end of the Foundation Stage.

(DCSF, 2008a)

The intentions of The EYFS are to achieve these aims by a principled approach to:

✓ setting standards;

✓ promoting equality of opportunity;

✓ creating a framework for partnership working;

✓ improving quality and consistency;

✓ laying a secure foundation for future learning and development.

(DCSF, 2008a)

There are four principled approaches to The Early Years Foundation Stage.

✓ Learning and Development: recognising the individual rhythms of children's development, and acknowledging that all areas of development are equally important and interconnected.

✓ A Unique Child: recognising that every child is a competent learner.

✓ Positive Relationships: emphasising the importance of loving, affectionate and secure relationships for children's well-being.

✓ Enabling Environments: emphasising the importance of the child's environment to the development and learning process.

(adapted from DCSF, 2008a p.9)

PRACTICAL TASK

The EYFS brings together existing policy documents to support children's development and learning. Consider the following.

1 How will your practice be influenced by the implementation of the EYFS?

2 How will this impact upon your current practice?

The introduction of the EYFS has raised the need for training in order to meet its requirements. Section 13 of the Childcare Act (2006) requires local authorities to secure the provision of information and to provide training, to support the Early Years workforce within the requirements of the EYFS. The EYFS is centralised and provides a single quality framework for Early Years practice. The training and implementation, however, is devolved at a local level. Local authorities are required to develop action plans based on local needs and priorities.

Early Years Professional Status

The impact of a range of policies, reforms and initiatives regarding the Early Years workforce has led to changes in the qualifications and training within the sector. Traditionally, the Early Years workforce was made up of people entering the sector with a variety of qualifications, backgrounds and experiences. The demands of the ECM, CAF and EYFS are for professionals to work together. The aim is to raise quality standards within the early years, and has led to the creation of a new professional role in the sector. The Children's Workforce Development Council, in an attempt to meet the EYFS requirements, introduced a set of standards and invested in creating a new graduate role the Early Years Professional Status. This is seen as the 'gold' standard, which attempts to ensure the implementation of EYFS and to improve quality in Early Years by meeting the outlined outcomes. Ofsted, the government body that inspects the education sector for standards of quality, will be introduced into the Early Years sector, and the outcomes that each child meet needs to be measurable.

The creation of the Early Years Professional role includes responsibilities to lead the practice across the EYFS in a range of settings. The local authorities are the main body responsible in administering this process. In order to achieve EYPS, candidates need to meet 39 standards, and to cover a range of skills that are organised under six headings.

The Standards: candidates for Early Years Professional Status should demonstrate through their practice . . .

Knowledge and understanding . . . *that a secure knowledge and understanding of the following underpins their own practice and informs their leadership of others*

S1   The principles and content of the Early Years Foundation Stage and how to put them in to practice

S2   The individual and diverse ways in which children develop and learn from birth to the end of the foundation stage and thereafter

S3   How children's well-being, development, learning and behaviour can be affected by a range of influences and transitions from both inside and outside the setting

S4   The main provisions of local and national statutory and non-statutory frameworks, within which children's services work, and their implications for Early Years settings

S5   The current legal requirements, national policies, guidance on health and safety, safeguarding, and promoting the well-being of children, and the implications of these for Early Years settings

S6   The contribution that other professionals within the setting and beyond can make to children's physical and emotional well-being, development and learning

Effective practice . . . *that they meet all the following Standards and that they can lead and support others to:*

S7 Have high expectations of all children and demonstrate a commitment to ensuring that they can achieve their full potential

S8 Establish and sustain a safe, welcoming, purposeful, stimulating and encouraging environment where children feel confident and secure, and are able to develop and learn

S9 Provide balanced and flexible daily and weekly routines that meet children's needs and enable them to develop and learn

S10 Use close, informed observation and other strategies to monitor children's activity, development and progress systematically and carefully, and to use this information to inform, plan and improve practice and provision

S11 Plan and provide safe and appropriate child-led and adult initiated experiences, activities and play opportunities in indoor, outdoor and out-of-setting contexts, which enable children to develop and learn

S12 Select, prepare and use a range of resources suitable for children's ages, interests and abilities, taking into account diversity, and therefore promoting equality and inclusion

S13 Make effective personalised provision for the children that they work with

S14 Respond appropriately to children, informed by how children develop and learn, and demonstrate a clear understanding of possible next steps in the child's development and learning

S15 Support the development of children's language and communication skills

S16 Engage in sustained shared thinking with children

S17 Promote positive behaviour, self-control and independence through using effective behaviour management strategies, and developing children's social, emotional and behavioural skills

S18 Promote children's rights, equality, inclusion and anti-discriminatory ethics in all aspects of their practice

S19 Establish a safe environment and employ practices that promote children's health, safety and physical, mental and emotional well-being

S20 Recognise when a child is in danger or is at risk of harm, and know how to act appropriately to protect them

S21 Assess, record and report on progress on children's development and learning, and to use this as a basis for differentiating provision

S22 Give constructive and sensitive feedback to help children understand what they have achieved, to think about what needs to done next and, when appropriate, encourage children to think about, evaluate and improve upon their own performance

S23 Identify and support children whose progress, development or well-being is affected by changes or difficulties in their personal circumstances, and know when to refer them to the relevant colleagues for specialist support

S24 Be accountable for the delivery of high quality provision

Relationships with children . . . *that they meet all the following Standards and that they can lead and support others to:*

S25 Establish fair, respectful, trusting, supportive and constructive relationships with children

S26 Communicate sensitively and effectively with children from birth to the end of the foundation stage

S27 Listen to children, pay attention to what they say, and to value and respect their views

S28 Demonstrate the positive values, attitudes and behaviour that they expect from children

Communicating and working in partnership with families and carers . . . *that they meet all the following Standards and that they can lead and support others to:*

S29 Recognise and respect the influential and enduring contribution that families and parents/carers can make to children's development, well-being and learning

S30 Establish fair, respectful, trusting and constructive relationships with families and parents/carers, and to communicate sensitively and effectively with them

S31 Work in partnership with families and parents/carers, at home and in the setting, to nurture children, in order to help them develop and to improve outcomes for them

S32 Provide formal and informal opportunities through which information about children's well-being, development and learning can be shared between the setting and with families and parents/carers

Teamwork and collaboration . . . *that they meet the following Standards:*

S33 Establish and sustain a culture of collaborative and cooperative working between colleagues

S34 Ensure that colleagues working with them understand their roles and are involved appropriately in helping children to meet planned objectives

S35 Influence and shape the policies and practices of the setting and to share in a collective responsibility for their implementation

S36 Contribute to the work of a multi-professional team and, where appropriate, coordinate and implement agreed programmes and interventions on a day-to-day basis

Professional development . . . *that they meet all the following Standards and that they can lead and support others to:*

S37 Develop and use skills in literacy, numeracy and information and communications technology to support their work with children and wider professional activities

S38 Reflect on and evaluate the impact of their practice, modifying approaches where necessary, and take responsibility for identifying and meeting their professional development needs

S39 Take a creative and constructively critical approach towards innovation, and adapt practice if its benefits and improvements can be identified

(Adapted from CWDC, 2007a pp. 7–8)

CWDC announced that in January 2007 the first cohort of 338 candidates achieved the EYPS. The CWDC also announced a commitment to the continuation of the EYPS, and a graduate-led Early Years profession to manage change and ensure improvement of quality in the Early Years.

The stated targets are as follows.

- 2010   6,200 graduates achieving EYPS;
- 2010   70 per cent of the workforce achieving a relevant Level 3 qualification;
- 2015   20,000 graduates achieving EYPS.

(CWDC, 2007)

To summarise, the Early Years Professionals Status is a standardised national award for experienced graduates who work in the Early Years sector. Although EYPS is equivalent to a teacher's qualification it does not have Qualified Teacher Status (QTS). To gain the EYPS, practitioners should demonstrate that they have met the Standards outlined above, and also have relevant experience of working with young children from 0–5 years. Training is followed by validation and candidates are assessed against all of the 39 Standards.

The role of the EYP in observation and assessment

As already indicated, the overall aim of the EYFS is to help young children to achieve the five outcomes of ECM. The EYFS creates a framework for parents and professionals to work together. Central to ECM is the CAF, which promotes a holistic approach to the assessment of children, and which strengthens partnerships between children's services and parents. Moreover, the Common Core of Skills and Knowledge (CWDC, 2007b) is of great importance in order to create a children's workforce which will be able to 'join up' to deliver the five outcomes of the ECM. Under the second heading of the Common Core skills, 'Child and Young Person', the first heading is 'Observation and Judgement'. Professionals should be able to to do the following.

- *Observe a child or young person's behaviour, understand its context, and notice any unexpected changes.*

- *Listen actively and respond to concerns expressed about developmental or behavioural changes.*

- *Record observations in an appropriate manner.*

- *Understand that babies, children and young people see and experience the world in different ways.*

- *Evaluate each situation, taking into consideration the individual, their circumstances and development issues.*

- *Be able to recognise the signs of a possible developmental delay.*

- *Be able to support children and young people with a developmental difficulty or disability, and understand that their families, parents and carers will also need support and reassurance.*

- *Make considered decisions on whether concerns can be addressed by providing or signposting additional sources of information or advice.*

- *Where you feel that further support is needed, know when to take action yourself and when to refer to managers, supervisors or other relevant professionals.*

- *Be able to distinguish between fact and opinion.*

(adapted from DfES, 2005)

There is a statutory requirement for practitioners working in the children's sector to observe children. On the one hand there is the CAF as a tool to assess children at an early stage, to help identify additional needs and to try to prevent something from going wrong.

On the other hand, in the Early Years within the EYFS (which aims to meet the ECM's five outcomes), assessment is important and statutory. There are 13 assessment scales that define the following early learning goals.

- personal , social and emotional development;

- communication, language and literacy;

- problem solving, reasoning and numeracy;

- knowledge and understanding of the world;

- physical development;

- creative development.

The Practice Guidance for the Early Years Foundation Stage describes detailed outlines in the 'Look, listen and note' sections. Practitioners are expected to:

- make systematic observations and assessments of each child's achievements, interests and learning styles;
- use these observations and assessments to identify learning priorities and to plan relevant and motivating learning experiences for each child;
- match their observations to the expectations of the early learning goals.

(Statutory Framework for the Early Years Foundation Stage, DCSF, 2008a, p.16)

Among the main roles and responsibilities of the EYP is the ability to act as a lead professional in cases where CAF is taking place, and thus be able to complete the assessment scales through constant observation of children, communicating these assessment profiles with parents and with local authorities (DCSF, 2008a). Consequently, there is a need within EYP training to ensure that candidates master observation skills and understand the assessment processes. Subsequently, this book aims to discuss observations to assist EYP candidates in meeting the requirements of training in this area, and to further their understanding of the role of observations.

Overview of the book

In the context of the changes in the Early Years sector and workforce, systematic observations and assessments play an important role within the Early Years workforce's portfolio of skills. This book discusses the role of observation in the Early Years environment as a tool for assessment for all Early Years professionals, in relation to current policies and initiatives. Observation as a skill is very important to all people working with children. This has been recognised strongly in all the recent policy changes, and is reflected in the Common Core of Skills and Knowledge and the EYP Standards. This book aims to help you further your understanding of what observation is.

The observation process is not isolated from the rest of your practice or from the educational programme as a whole. It is interlinked with your practice and it helps you to develop your practice and your understanding of it.

This introductory chapter offers an overview of the current policies and the context that you will find yourself working in. In Chapter 1 issues around the views of the child which influence our pedagogy and practice in the Early Years are described and inform the issues covered in Chapter 2. In Chapter 2 the role of observation is discussed in relation to current legislation, and in relation to the everyday practice of an Early Years setting. Chapter 3 presents commonly-used observation techniques, with some practical examples for you to consider. It also discusses how observation recordings can be analysed. This is an important process, as interpretation of your findings will form your assessment of a child. In Chapter 4 the ethics of the observation process are explored in relation to the documentation of your findings, as an integral part of ethical procedures and considerations. How you document your information and with whom you share it is directed by regulations and informs good practice. Having built a theoretical understanding of the observations, Chapter 5 looks at some practical examples for observing children that focus on their development. In the light of a good understanding of the observation process, the final chapter discusses the role of the Early Years Professional, and draws conclusions as to the importance of observation skills for Early Years practice.

Department for Children, School and Families (2008b) *Practice Guidance for the Early Years Foundation Stage: Setting the Standards for Learning, Development, and Care for Children from birth to five*, Nottingham: DCSF.

Alternatively you can access Early Years Foundation Stage from http://www.standards.dcsf.gov.uk/eyfs/

The Statutory Framework for The Early Years Foundation Stage can be accessed from http://www.standards.dcsf.gov.uk/eyfs/resources/downloads/statutory-framework.pdf

Fitzgerald, D. and Kay, J. (2008) *Working together in children's services*, London: Routledge.

Nurse, A. (2007) *The new early years professional*, London: Routledge.

Useful websites

http://www.everychildmatters.gov.uk/uncrc/

http://www.victoria-climbie-inquiry.org.uk/

http://www.everychildmatters.gov.uk/deliveringservices/caf/

http://www.cwdcouncil.org.uk/projects/earlyyears.htm

integratedworking@cwdcouncil.org.uk

1 The pedagogy of Early Years

CHAPTER OBJECTIVES

By the end of this chapter you should:
- understand the child in context and how this influences Early Years practice;
- have developed an understanding of developmental theories;
- have developed a critical approach to Early Years pedagogy;
- have explored different curriculum practices.

This chapter addresses the following Standards for EYPS: S1, S27, S38 and S39.

Introduction

The introduction of Every Child Matters, the Common Assessment Framework and the Early Years Foundation Stage were welcomed by the Early Years sector. These policies aim to improve quality in the field of Early Years care and education, as well as raising standards, and bringing about a common quality framework for learning goals, activities and educational programmes. The Early Years Foundation Stage is very prescriptive of Early Years practice and is an outcomes-driven approach to pedagogy for practitioners. In order to be able to develop a critical approach to the EYFS, this chapter will:

- discuss different views and perspectives of childhood that influence Early Years pedagogy;

- explore the main developmental theories that influence our understanding of child development;

- analyse the pedagogical principles of EYFS;

- offer examples from two well-known approaches in order for you to be able to reflect on your own practice: namely, Reggio Emilia and Te Whaariki.

Views on childhood: an overview

In recent years research in the field of child development has become increasingly concerned with applying its vast knowledge base to the educational environment, and in creating a pedagogy for children. Today we know much more than ever before about the family, the school, and the community contexts that foster the development of physically, emotionally and socially healthy, cognitively competent and socially mature children. More than ever before children are actively involved in the decision-making processes and assessments that influence their lives and experiences.

The way societies perceive childhood impacts upon our approaches to children. The Early Years policy services and curricula reflect current perspectives of the child within society, and therefore inform our pedagogy. Looking at the social construction of childhood, there is a plethora of different readings about children that influence Early Years practice. Benton (1996), looking at how children are portrayed within the arts and in literature, describes seven types of child.

- The polite child

- The impolite child

- The innocent child

- The sinful child

- The authentic child

- The sanitised child

- The holy child.

David (1993) discusses the work of Dahlberg (1991), who argued that the ways in which different societies define childhood for their young overlay physiological constraints with their own concepts – or models – of how children should be at certain stages of their lives. David (1993) distinguishes two views: the 'child-as-being' view, where children are left to 'be children', and the 'child-as-project', where their lives are mapped out for them.

She comments that both views leave children at a loss; on the one hand, children are not prepared for the expectations of school and society, and on the other they are under pressure to achieve (David, 1993). These two views appear to be meaningful in our society, a society that demands from children so many skills, especially during schooling, and also later when approaching adult life.

Hendrick (1997), examining the social constructions of childhood in Britain since the end of the eighteenth century, suggests nine views of childhood, reflecting on the socio-economical, theological, political and historical changes within British society.

- The natural child

- The romantic child

- The evangelical child

- The child as child

- The schooled child

- The 'child-study' child

- Children of the nation

- The psychological child

- The child of the welfare state.

(Hendrick, 1997)

Finally, Mills and Mills (2000), in a more recent review of the literature on perspectives of childhood, suggest that there are several more possible views of childhood.

- Children as innocent

- Children as apprentices

- Children as people in their own right

- Children as members of a distinct group

- Children as vulnerable

- Children as animals.

They emphasise that 'in reality they [the views of child] cannot be isolated [from each other] but they are interlinked and overlapping' (p.9).

In order to help you reflect on your own views of childhood which might influence your practice, in the following paragraphs an overview of the dominant perspectives of childhood is presented.

The innocent child

The view of the child as innocent, and consequently in need of protection from the evils of society, is a view that was formed by Rousseau's philosophical ideas of childhood and was reinforced by theological considerations. Within this idea the child is viewed as being in need of protection and also representing a force for good. Adults are to take responsibility to ensure that the child is raised outside of the 'evil' influence of society.

Preparing the child for adulthood

This is the view of the child as an apprentice for adulthood, in which the child is being trained in order to be prepared for adult life. Within this view the child is being prepared to become a responsible adult. There is an emphasis on training for the child. Such training might include social skills, communication skills and vocational education.

The socially active child

This is a view of the child as a social person, capable of acting in the social world and of creating and sustaining their own culture. An extended view of this is of the child as a member of a distinct group. This view implies that the child needs a loving and secure environment in order to develop personally, socially and emotionally. When a child grows up in care, for example, then this needs to be in an environment where there are conditions for affection and for moral and material security.

The developmental child

This is a view of the child from a developmental perspective, where he or she passes through stages; for example, psychological stage theories such as Piagetian stages, or psychoanalytical stages.

The field of psychology determines the view of the developmental child where traditionally education seeks to further its understanding of children. Moreover, Early Years education has been based on developmental views of how children learn. An examination of the EYFS and Every Child Matters will reveal that the learning goals reflect these views.

The child in need of protection

The child is viewed as being in need of protection and is vulnerable. In some ways this reflects an emerging view of the child as a potential victim. Examining all the current policies regarding children there is an emphasis on protecting children from harm, keeping children safe and in promoting children's well-being.

As Early Years care and education is not isolated from the wider cultural and social context of our views of childhood, the pedagogy of Early Years is influenced by our views. The policy and the curricula are determined by our notions of childhood and reflect these views.

REFLECTIVE TASK

Considering the different views of childhood, can you reflect on your own upbringing, and consider which views might have shaped your own education. Share your experiences with your fellow students.

As a professional, which views do you think influence your practice?

An overview of theories on child development

Just as our views of childhood are influenced by historical, economic and cultural changes, similarly modern theories of child development have roots extending far into the past. For example, in medieval times children were regarded as miniature adults, a view called 'preformationism' (Aries, 1962). According to Aries (1962) childhood was not a distinct period of life, and this can be seen from the fact that children did not have clothes made specifically for them, nor were they provided with toys or given different activities from adults. As soon as children were sufficiently independent they were entering adult life and joining the adult workforce.

By the sixteenth century childhood was identified as a distinct phase of life. However, the dominant Puritan concept of original sin led to a harsh philosophy when it came to rearing children. There was a need to train the child, in order to help the child to be 'cleansed' of original sin. Enlightenment brought ideas favouring a more humane treatment of children (Berk, 1997), with an emphasis on children's education. Locke's *tabula rasa* statement of 1692, in which children were viewed as a blank slate that could be educated and shaped in any way that adults wanted, provided the basis for twentieth-century behaviourism, whilst Rousseau's (1911) notion of the child as 'noble savage' foreshadowed the concepts of stage and maturation.

A century later, Darwin's theory of evolution stimulated a scientific approach to the study of the child. The great revolution in research into child development occurred in the 1930s and 1940s (Dixon and Learner, 1992). Darwin's theory was the origin of the ethnology theory, which is concerned with the adaptive (or survival) value of behaviour (Lorenz and Tinbergen, in Dewsberry, 1992).

Child guidance professionals turned to the field of psychology in order to further their understanding of how children develop and learn. The following paragraphs discuss the dominant psychological theories in the field of child development and learning.

Psychoanalytical theory

The psychoanalytical theory is dominated by the work of two main theorists, Sigmund Freud and Erik Erikson. Both are read widely and influence the way that we think about children today.

Sigmund Freud's theory challenged the view of the child as innocent, provoking a debate about children's experiences, and how these experiences subsequently shape children's personalities. The main emphasis in Freud's theory was placed on development being driven by aggressive and sexual instincts (Freud, 1923, 1933). He developed a psychosexual theory that formulated different stages of psychosexual development. Freud (1964) believed that sex is the most important instinct in human development. In his view the different activities that a baby undertakes – such as sucking the thumb or a child breaking rules – are activities that relate to the child's psychosexual development. Freud did not view sex in childhood from an erotic perspective. Instead, he believed that when children develop and move through different stages, the focus of the sex instinct moves through different parts of their bodies. Thus Freud's 'stages' are related to parts of the human body.

He suggested that children move through five psychosexual stages during which three components of personality are developed: the 'id', 'ego', and 'superego'. When babies are born the 'id' is already present and it helps the new-born to satisfy basic biological needs. For example, when a baby is hungry he or she cries for food. The ego is related to the consciousness and reflects the child's abilities to learn, reason and remember. When a baby is hungry, for example, he or she can remember how to receive food and waits for his or her bottle. The final component of the personality is the 'superego', and this starts developing between the age of two-and-a-half to three years of age. The superego is related to moral values, and is the internalisation of these moral values and received rules (Freud, 1933).

Erik Erikson was a Freudian student who did not agree with Freud's emphasis on the sexual instinct. He modified Freud's theory by taking into consideration the environment that children grow up in. Erikson (1963, 1982) introduced the idea of cultural and social influences upon human development. He suggested that children must cope with 'social realities' in order to develop appropriate patterns of behaviour. Erikson placed an important role on the social environment, and hence he suggested his own eight stages of psychosocial development. He believed (Erikson, 1963) that human beings develop through eight 'crises' (or psychosocial stages) during their lives. Each of these stages is related to biological development, and to social and cultural interactions at certain times of our lives.

Both Freud and Erikson offered us a detailed account of children's personal, social and emotional development. In the field of developmental psychology the psychoanalytical theory was criticised as limited, in terms of suitably explaining a child's development and learning comprehensively. Although both theorists had a significant influence on the study of children's development (Tyson and Tyson, 1990), they do not offer us an adequate explanation of *how* and *why* this development takes place (Shaffer and Kipp, 2007).

Behaviourism

Behaviourism changed ways of thinking in developmental psychology. The behaviouristic school of psychology placed a lot of emphasis on observations. Theorists within the school of behaviourism – such as Watson, Pavlov and Skinner, who formed the main ideas of this theory – developed scientific ways of observing in order to understand development.

The main principles of behaviourism can be summarised by the following.

- Human behaviour, especially social behaviour, is acquired rather than inborn.

- Emphasis on the role of environmental stimuli.

- A focus on learning. Learning is defined as 'changes in behaviour which occur as the result of experience and interactions with the environment'. (Glassman, 2000)

This theory offers a detailed account of how human beings learn. It has contributed to furthering our understanding of children's development and learning, and offered a scientific approach to the observation of children.

However, it does not consider the social and cultural context of human beings. Among the theorists who criticised behaviorism for taking little account of the cognitive and socio-cultural factors that influence human development, is Bandura, who proposed a social learning theory as an alternative to behaviourism.

Social cognition

Albert Bandura (1971, 1977, 1986, 1989, 2001) argued that human beings develop by using their cognitive abilities in the social and cultural environment in which they live. He suggested the idea of observational learning as an important aspect for development: human beings develop and learn by the examples of others. Children make sense of the world and learn how to behave in particular moments of their lives through observing others (e.g. parents, teachers and other children). Bandura elaborates on this idea with examples of children being violent. He presented to young children, in a controlled laboratory setting, an adult beating a doll. The children were then invited to go into a room and play with this doll and with other toys that were there. Observing children's responses, he demonstrated that children imitated what the adult did, when they bit the doll. Bandura concluded, consequently, that children continuously learn behaviours through the observation of others.

Although Bandura studied development as part of the environment, he did not simply provide a limited description of the environment as an influential factor in human development.

Ecology

In contrast to Bandura, Urie Bronfenbrenner (1977, 1979, 1989, 1995, 2005), the originator of ecological systems theory, viewed the natural environment as the most influential factor upon human development. He challenged theorists that study human development and learning in artificial and laboratory contexts, and proposed the study of human development within the natural environment. He defined an 'environment' as being 'a set of nested structures, each inside the next, like a set of Russian dolls' (1979, p.22). As a result he viewed the child as developing within a complex system of relationships, affected by the multiple levels of the surrounding environment – such as immediate settings to broad cultural values, laws and customs.

His main idea of how children develop as part of systems is illustrated in the following figure on page 21.

As Figure 1.1 illustrates, 'the nested structures' are systems.

- Microsystem (the closet environment of the child such as parents and grandparents, family friends).

- Mesosystem (the immediate environment that relates to family such as neighbourhood, school).

- Exosystem (the different settings that might influence a child's development, such as parents working environments, cultural groups, religious groups that parents belong to).

- Macrosystem (the wider socio-economic, political, cultural and legal contexts).

For Bronfenbrenner, human development involves interactions of these four systems – the micro, meso, exo and macrosystems over time. This approach to child development emphasises the children as active participants in creating their own environments and their experiences of their interactions with the social context of a child as important aspects of human development.

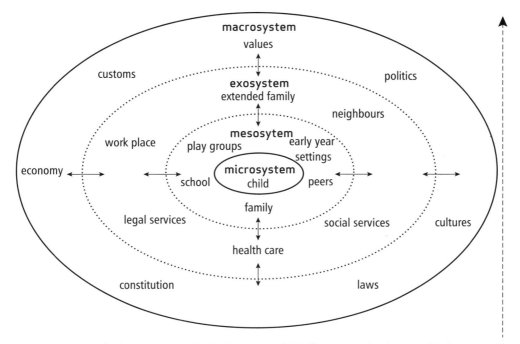

Figure 1.1 Bronfenbrenner's ecological system which illustrates the layers of influence in a child's life

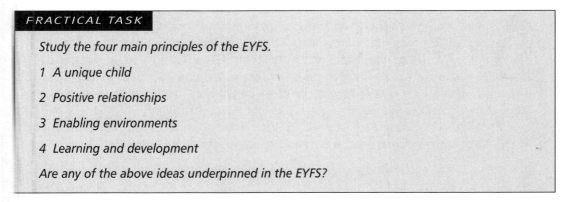

PRACTICAL TASK

Study the four main principles of the EYFS.

1 A unique child

2 Positive relationships

3 Enabling environments

4 Learning and development

Are any of the above ideas underpinned in the EYFS?

Cognition

In developmental psychology the school of cognitive psychology has been one of the most dominant theories in child development. Cognition is concerned with the 'study of the processes involved in cognition – the processes involved in making sense of the environment and interacting appropriately with it' (Eysenck, 1995, p.10). The mental processes through which we attempt to understand the world were defined as:

* thinking and knowing;

* reasoning;

- learning;

- problem solving;

- using language;

- memory;

- perception.

The two most important theorists who have furthered our understanding of child development in cognitive psychology are Jean Piaget – who emphasised that a child has an active mind inhabited by rich structures of knowledge – and Lev Vygotsky. Vygotsky's socio-cognitive perspectives (1986) focused on how cultural values, beliefs, customs and social interactions are necessary for children in acquiring new ways of thinking.

Piaget

Piaget's theory suggests that children develop through stages. Children develop and construct knowledge (schema) via these stages. According to Piaget (1929, 1952, 1954, 1962, 1968, 1969), the schemata, which are specific psychological structures, change with age. Piaget's cognitive theory suggests that during the first two years of life, cognition can be seen in the baby's motor actions towards the environment.

To explain how children acquire schemata and subsequently change these, Piaget identifies two important intellectual functions: assimilation and accommodation. Assimilation is the process by which the child cognitively adapts to, and organises, the environment, and which therefore allows growth but not a change of schemata. The process responsible for changes in schemata is accommodation. Accommodation is the part of the process of adaptation, in which old schemata are adjusted and new ones are created to produce a better fit within the environment. The processes of assimilation and accommodation are necessary for cognitive development. For Piaget, these two processes interact in a balanced way, and he calls that interaction 'equilibrium'. This is a self-regulatory process whose tools are assimilation and accommodation. Children with equilibrium transfer external experiences into internal structures (or 'schemata').

It is not until the end of the second year that children begin to use mental-symbolic processes in order to adapt to their environment (Piaget, 1952). Piaget (1952) made clear that the behaviour of small infants, although not conceptually based, was nevertheless intelligent. By this he meant that infants had ways of meeting their needs, of using their own resources and other resources in the environment, and of adapting those resources to the specific nature of the task at hand. This sensory motor intelligence was embodied not in the mind, but in the actions and movements that the baby made in direct interaction with its environment (Piaget, 1952, 1962). There follows the move into childhood and into pre-operational thought. The distinguishing characteristic between infancy and childhood is the use of language and the ability to perform logical reasoning.

Another characteristic that assists development from infancy to childhood is the 'object concept', or the concept of 'object permanence'. This refers to a set of implicit, common-sensical beliefs that we all share about the basic nature and behaviour of objects, including ourselves. When an object disappears from one's sight, adults do not assume that it has thereby gone out of existence, but this skill does not exist from the beginning of our life and is acquired only gradually. When children acquire object permanence it is then when symbolic representation involves implications for language, attention and for social development.

According to Piaget knowledge is not absorbed passively from the environment, but is constructed through interactions and experiences between the mental structures (schemata) and the environment. As a result, knowledge is constructed from a child's actions in the environment. In Piaget's theory there are three kinds of knowledge.

✓ physical

✓ logical-mathematical

✓ social

The Piagetian theory has had a great impact on the Early Years environment. The developmentally appropriate practices in the Early Years settings, and the pedagogical principles that have evolved as a result of his theory, have changed the ways that learning in the Early Years is viewed.

For example, the physical environment of the classroom has changed within the last few decades. The classroom design itself provides a context for the child, and is now the dominant layout for an Early Years class. There is a cultural richness in Early Years classes, where a wealth of real life experiences is transferred into the environment. There are carpets where children can relax, library areas where children can have their first experiences of reading, corners such as a sand area, construction areas with Lego blocks, 'post offices', etc. These further a child's understanding of the world, and they are the learning opportunities that the Early Years class is offering to children, in order to construct and facilitate knowledge.

The following description presents a picture of a classroom that fosters development and promotes learning, and is influenced by Piagetian ideas.

CASE STUDY

Example of a physical environment of a classroom which applies Piaget's theories

The classroom is divided into small learning areas, where groups of children may play with sand or occupy themselves in parallel or co-operative play with bricks, Lego, or painting, while others are supported by the Early Years professional in a group task. Others are engaged in symbolic play or dramatic play. A few children may be at the writing area. One or two are on the floor looking at a big picture book, or sitting in a chair in the library corner looking at or reading books, leading, perhaps, to a shared reading with an educator or a peer.

Outside, children may be involved with larger materials and apparatus in solitary or co-operative imaginative play, or with others in socially-agreed play. Children may be painting at an easel or writing. The Early Years professionals move between the various activities, supporting children with their experience of the materials. Occasionally, usually at the start or the end of the session, the class comes together for a group story reading, a shared book experience or a song. Thus, a whole range of activities will be taking place.

Vygotsky

While Piaget viewed cognitive development as the result of the individual child's interaction with the environment, Vygotsky (1986, 1962) expands further on that view. Vygotsky emphasised the importance of social interaction for children's cognitive development. He introduced the idea of the 'zone of proximal development' (or 'ZPD'). Vygotsky (1986) identifies 'the zone of actual development' which 'defines actions that have already matured; that is, the end of product of development'. This refers to a number of skills that a child has already mastered and which help the child to achieve certain tasks. However, during development children are in the zone of proximal development where the potential development of a child is situated. '[Children] that have not yet matured but are in the process of maturation functions that will mature tomorrow, but are currently in an embryonic state' (Vygotsky, 1986, p.87). This refers to a range of skills that the child cannot yet handle, but with the help of a more mature or skilled peer or an adult, the child can master these skills. In practice, this means that children need social interaction. The help of an adult, or other children, is an important and integral part of a child's development.

In Vygotsky's theory there is emphasis on what children *can* do rather than what they *cannot* do. Consequently, in Vygotksy's theory learning is constructed as a partnership between the child and the adult.

ZPD with the help of an adult

The following example attempts to demonstrate how the interaction of the Early Years professional with the child helps the child to read a picture book. The book is about animals. At the end of each page there is some push-button music relating to the sound of the animal illustrated in the picture.

CASE STUDY *continued*

EYP:	*Do you want to look at this book with me?*
George:	*(He just nods his head.)*
EYP:	*So, do you want to look at the book?*
George:	*Yes.*
EYPS:	*(reads the story) 'On the farm the little dog. . .'*
	(George interrupts the reading and presses a button to listen to the music.)
EYP:	*We have not reached the part where you must press the button for the music. Do you want to wait? It is not going to take long.*
	(George looks at the EYP and presses the button again.)
EYP:	*Do you want me to suggest something to you, then? We can do the following: I will give you the book for you to turn the pages and listen to all the noises, and then, if you want, we can still look at it together.*
	(George takes the book and starts to press the button more than three times.)
EYP:	*You know, if we turn the page like this you should be able to listen to some more nice sounds. Shall we do it like this? (Taking the book gently from George's hand and turning the page slowly.)*
	(George sees the new button and presses it. He presses it about three times and then turns the next page by himself, discovers the button and starts the next piece of music playing.)

After he has experienced the whole book, the EYP asks George if he still wants to look at the book and read it. In this way George discovered that he had to press the buttons in order to listen to the music – the same way in which he learnt how to turn the pages. This happened with some help.

Example 2: ZPD with the help of a more experienced peer.

Another example of ZPD is illustrated in the following extract. In this one it is a mature peer who offers help to another child:

Sophia, Raj and Anka were in the library corner with a large number of books. They were looking at the pictures.

The Early Years professional said that it was 'tidy-up time', so all three of them started to put the books and the newspapers back in their places, according to the symbols that had been designed to categorise the different types of books and magazines.

CASE STUDY *continued*

Tidiness is not simply the act of shelving books back in the library, but putting them back according to their themes. These were represented by the use of small pictures: the labels bore different symbols for storybooks, knowledge books, fantasy books, talking books, magazines, and so on.

   📖   *Storybooks*

   ▤   *Talking books*

   🗁   *Magazines*

Raj: *This is a magazine – it goes with the magazines, next to hairdresser's shop, and this one goes here with the storybooks.*

Anka: *What about this one?*

Sophia: *This is a storybook and goes. . . oh yes. . . here, where the symbol for 'books' is.*

Anka: *Oh! Here's another one (Anka picks up a Talking Book and puts it in the right place).*

To summarise, both Piaget and Vygotsky are important because they challenge educators to rethink childhood cognitive development. They further our understanding of how children think, develop and learn, offering us a view that young children are more capable than we perhaps had once assumed. Both theorists placed an emphasis on what children can do, and they viewed learning not only as construction of knowledge, but as an ability to use that knowledge and to apply it appropriately in different contexts. They changed the ways in which we consider children's abilities. As a result we can offer a more enriched environment to young children, full of activities and support that enhance their own development and their learning.

In the following example from an Early Years setting try to investigate whether you can identify any of the ideas of Piaget and Vygotsky's theories in practice.

Activity: Planting beans

The Early Years Professional introduced the activity and the diary to a small group of children. They had to write down who put water on the beans and when, and to chart the beans' development through making drawings. Then, with the assistance of the adults, the children started to fill in the notebook according to their daily observations. Every day the group was asked to spend about five minutes checking on the beans, and then to record their observations in the notebook. In the second week after the planting, when the children had finished checking the plants, the children went to the writing area and occupied themselves there. When they had finished they came back to the Early Years professional. The child in the following extract wanted to write down her name on her drawing, but did not know how, and so she approached the EYP.

C1:   Can you write down my name?

EYP: What have you done in your drawing?

C1:   I draw what I see in the beans.

EYP: So what do you say, then?

C1:   That this bean (points to the big blue shapes similar to a circle on her drawing) has grown so big. Here it is (pointing to her drawing). I wrote my own letters.

EYP: And what do these letters say?

C1:   (As if reading) 'The bean is big'. This is my gardening notebook. Can you write my name?

EYP: What are the sounds of your name?

C1:   Lisa

EYP: What is the first one?

C1:   Lisa

EYP: What is the first one you can hear?

C1:   'L'?

EYP: Yes. Let's write down the letter 'L'.

Comment

During this activity we can see Piaget's idea that children learn actively through interaction with the actual plants (the real world is transferred into the class), and they were able to construct a product/knowledge/schema with real life examples as a context. Children were given roles and responsibilities, and through this activity a context was provided for children in order to learn how the plants develop.

In the dialogue with the EYP and the child we can identify the input of the EYP to help the child in creating her own notebook and to link sounds to letters.

Within the dialogue above the zone of proximal development can be identified. The child discusses her request with the Early Years Professional, and through the guidance of the adult the child has begun to make sense of letters as symbols.

Recent perspectives

The field of child development continues to seek new directions. Information-processing views the development of the mind as a symbol-manipulating system through which information flows (Klahr, 1992). This approach helps researchers to achieve a clear understanding of what children of different ages do when faced with tasks and problems. New technological achievements in the medical field, such as MRI technology, have helped neuroscience to understand how the brain develops and functions. There is more evidence available now to explain how parts of the brain are used when a child faces a task or a problem.

Comparing these child development theories, we can conclude that they differ in many respects. The main focus is on different aspects of development and all use observations as their main tool to study children. The psychoanalytical theory emphasises children's social and emotional development. Piaget's cognitive theory, information-processing, and Vygotsky's socio-cultural theory, stress important changes in children's thinking. They are investigating child development in the context of a non-isolated environment and regard the child as an active learner through experience and interaction with that environment – both early and later experiences are important. The remaining approaches – behaviourism and ecological systems theory – discuss factors assumed to affect all aspects of a child's functioning.

Considering the influence of these theories in the field of Early Years education and care, they can offer a perspective of the child-as-learner, where learning is determined by the child's own development.

REFLECTIVE TASK

Reflect on your own practice and consider what developmental theories influence your practice.

Conditions for learning

Learning is not an activity that occurs in isolation. One of the main principles of the EYFS is to develop an enabling environment for children's learning and development. The Early Years setting should not be separated from wider cultural and social contexts. Although the Early Years professional is working with a national quality framework (the EYFS), he or she should look to develop local conditions for learning that apply to the needs of the immediate setting, and which take the environment into consideration.

In such a learning environment certain skills are not developed in isolation. Piaget viewed human development as an integrated process where feelings, emotions and relationships have an effect on cognitive skills, such as numeracy and literacy. Learning in the Early Years is the product of many experiences in meaningful contexts.

In designing educational programmes and activities for children the following conditions should be considered:

Emphasis on children's development

The development of a child is central in Early Years practice. Within the EYFS the learning goals are set around children's development.

✓ Personal, social and emotional development

✓ Communication, language and literacy

✓ Problem solving, reasoning and numeracy

✓ Knowledge and understanding of the world

✓ Physical development

✓ Creative development

Emphasis on play

Play is important in early years. Within the EYFS again there is a lot of emphasis on play. The EYFS describes play as 'purposeful'. In an attempt to understand this we need to ask 'What is play'?

Moyles (1989) defines 'play' as the situation 'when children do their learning'. Play is when children have opportunities to express their thoughts and emotions, to try out new things and possibilities, to put different elements of a situation together in various ways, and to look at problems from different viewpoints (Bruner, 1972). An important element of play is pleasure. Children need play to enjoy themselves, as well as to enrich their experiences whilst interacting with their environment. Play for young children should not been seen as a separate activity that children do at a specific time. It is something that very young children, in particular, do consistently. Consequently, play is oriented by spontaneity. Early forms of play in very young children lack any organisation and are used by children to help them make sense of the world, to communicate with others, and to explore their environment.

PRACTICAL TASK

In the following extracts of children's play can you identify any of the characteristics of play?

Example 1:

Fay and Peter were playing in the construction area with the cars:

Fay: I will go to the supermarket to buy some petrol for my car.

Peter: I will give you the keys.

Fay: Yes, where are they?

Peter: Here *(gives her a Lego brick)*.

Fay: *I will bring some milk for the tea.*

Example 2

Mary and Helen were in the hairdresser's area and pretending to dry their hair.

Mary: *I think we should straighten our hair now.*

Helen: *OK, let's use these. (Helen hands Mary two pens pretending that they are straighteners)*

(Mary picks up a brush pretending that it is the dryer.)

Helen: *What are you doing? That is a brush. Take the hair dryer. It's behind the mirror. (She picks up an empty plastic bottle and gives it to Mary.)*

Mary: *Thank you. Do you have any gel?*

Helen: *Yes, here it is (picks up an empty bottle and gives it to Mary).*

Emphasis on children's needs

Children's needs are an important factor that influence children's learning. These derive from developmental needs such as physical activities, social and emotional well-being, and opportunities for play.

Emphasis on children's freedom to choose materials and activities

The importance of children's participation has been emphasised in a number of policies relating to children, such as the 'United Nations Rights for the Child' and 'Every Child Matters' document. The enabling of children as active learners, who are able to take control of their own learning and development, requires an environment where children are given the appropriate opportunities to participate in choosing their own materials and activities.

Emphasis on children's ownership of their learning

Similarly, children should be given opportunities to explore their own learning. Children should not be underestimated in terms of their abilities to translate their interests into activities, and thus to explore the world. Children's internal needs drive them to form relationships with other children and adults, and in forming these relationships they discover new ways of learning.

Pedagogy in practice

Developing a pedagogy for Early Years requires the construction of a professional identity for early years. Within this process it is important for the Early Years professional to have a good understanding of a variety of developmental theories, as well as pedagogical practices, and an understanding of children's developmental needs.

However, the Early Years Professional has to work within a context. Miller, et al. (2003), comparing different curricula across the time line and in other countries, found that 'curricular guidance for the Early Years has become increasingly centralised in a number of countries' (p.113). Again, the Early Years Professional is asked to be able to work creatively and to improve practice in the Early Years sector.

This is a difficult task for the Early Years Professional. It requires a very good understanding of current policies and practices, such as EYFS. In your search for pedagogy in the Early Years it is important to look at other pedagogical practices to further one's understanding. In studying other effective practices you should not seek to transfer them to your own practice without adaptation, but adopt a critical approach in order to compare and reflect on your own practice, and also to enrich your understanding of Early Years pedagogy.

The following paragraphs provide an overview of the EYFS and two further effective curricula.

Early Years Foundation Stage

When we discuss the development of a pedagogy for the Early Years the starting point is a search for quality within it. In the EYFS there is an attempt to set the standards for Early Years practice and the aim is to improve quality. Early Years practice is viewed as a partnership between the settings and the parents. The ultimate aim of the EYFS is a standardised practice among Early Years settings, with parents being assured 'that essential standards of provision are in place' (DCSF, 2008a, p.10).

In order to provide quality in Early Years education, it is important for professionals and practitioners to understand children's development. To achieve this, some main principles are recommended in the EYFS.

✓ A Unique Child recognises that every child is a competent learner from birth who can be resilient, capable, confident and self-assured. There is a commitment to focus around development, inclusion, health and safety, and well-being.

✓ Positive Relationships describes how children learn to be strong and independent, from a base of loving and secure relationships with parents and /or a key person. These commitments are based on respect, partnerships with parents, supporting learning, and in identifying the role of the key person.

✓ Enabling Environments explains that the environment plays a key role in supporting and extending a child's development and learning. The commitments are focused around observation, assessment and planning; support for every child; the learning environment; and, in the wider context, transitions, continuity and multi-agency working.

✓ Learning and Development recognises that children develop and learn in different ways and at different speeds, and that all areas of learning and development are as equally important and inter-connected.

Within these views the EYFS attempts to adopt a holistic approach to Early Years care and education with a focus on developmental areas. The EYFS offers detailed guidelines for Early Years practice. Within the EYFS framework it is important that the Early Years Professional is able to implement these practices and form a theoretical argument regarding his/her own practice and pedagogical values.

To summarise, the role of the EYP in the Early Years learning environment should be:

• to lead practice based on a theoretical background;

• to stimulate pedagogical discussion among the team, and to do so requires an understanding of current pedagogical practices;

• to disseminate and implement current policies within the team.

Reggio Emilia

Reggio Emilia is a community-supported system of early childhood education and care situated in a small town in northern Italy. Loris Malaguzzi introduced an Early Years system to the Reggio Emilia province, based on his vision of a child as an active, strong, and powerful human being. Both Malaguzzi (1995) and his co-worker Rinaldi (1995) based their pedagogy on cognitive ideas of child development. They placed particular emphasis on Vygotsky's ideas, that knowledge is not adopted by the child, but is constructed by the child through interaction with a more mature or experienced peer or adult (Miller *et al.*, 2003).

The originality of Reggio Emilia is that there is no written curriculum. Instead it takes a localised approach to the education of its young children. This approach is free from external and formalised pressures and standards. There are no government objectives or goals to be achieved, and the starting point is the child; consequently the curriculum 'emerges' from children's own interests and needs (Rinaldi, 1995). The Reggio Emilia approach to Early Years pedagogy is developed via a constant dialogue with the Early Years team, the children and the parents. In this approach the child is viewed as 'rich in potential, strong, powerful, competent and, most of all connected to adults and other children' (Malaguzzi, 1993, p.10).

The view of the child 'rich in potential' underpins the main principles of this pedagogical approach. Learning is viewed as a social activity that involves all participants: parents, children and the local community. Consequently, all of these participants are engaging themselves in constant discussion about the activities in the classes.

Fundamental principles in the Reggio Emilia approach to Early Years pedagogy are:

- the partnerships with parents and communication with them;

- listening to the 'hundred languages' that children use to communicate;

- informal assessment and documentation of children's work as the starting point for the discussion among staff, children and parents;

- the physical environment is important in the Reggio Emilia for the emotional stability of the children.

In the Reggio Emilia approach, the Early Years workforce collects evidence about what the children are involved in. This evidence is documented either in the form of individual portfolios for each child or by photographs, and these become starting points for discussions at weekly team meetings. From these discussions the planning of activities emerges. Ongoing dialogue among the staff, parents, children and the wider community forms the education programme and its activities – this being an important and key aspect in the pedagogy of Reggio Emilia.

Miller et al. (2003) citing Fillipini (1995) illustrates how Reggio Emilia works:

The 'pedagogista' (or 'Early Years Professional') works with the parents and teachers towards educational aims and goals and has a coordinating role with many facets, including administration and training.

And again, citing Vecchi (1995):

The 'atelierista' (or 'artist in residence') is closely involved in project work and in the visual documentation of the children's work.

Te Whaariki

In the Early Years settings in New Zealand there is an attempt to create a multicultural curriculum for the early years. This is known as 'Te Whaariki', and is an attempt to describe the nature of the national curriculum. Based on Bronfenbrenner's ideas about the 'nested environment' and human development it contains, as a main principle, the inclusion of beliefs, values and cultural identities of each local community (New Zealand Ministry of Education, 1996).

The Te Whaariki curriculum is based on an emphasis on children's freedom to choose materials and activities, and to take ownership of their own learning. The child is viewed thus:

To grow up as competent and confident learners and communicators, healthy in mind, body, and spirit, secure in their sense of belonging and in the knowledge that they make a valued contribution to society. (New Zealand Ministry of Education, 1996)

The framework of this curriculum is based on children's own interests and aspirations (Tyler, 2002). Similarly to the EYFS, there are some principles to guide the Early Years team.

33

- Empowerment (*Whakamana*). It is central to the curriculum that the child takes ownership of their own development and learning.

- Holistic development (*Kotahitanga*). The child is viewed as a 'whole'. It is emphasised that the child learns in a holistic way, taking into consideration not only the child's physical, social, emotional and cognitive development, but also the cultural context and the spiritual aspects of the child's environment.

- Family and Community (*Whanau Tangata*). Again, similar to the EYFS partnership, the wider world of family and community is an integral part of early childhood curriculum.

- Relationships (*Nga Hononga*). Children's interactions with peers, adults and real life objects that enhance children's learning.

Teachers using the Te Whaariki framework take into account children's well-being, their sense of belonging, the contributions they make, the importance of communication, and opportunities to develop exploration. Furthermore, within this curriculum framework there is an importance placed on a Maori immersion within the New Zealand curriculum in order to strengthen 'Te Reo Maori' – the Maori language. Te Whaariki recognises the distinctive role of an identifiable Maori curriculum that protects Maori culture through the use of Maori language (Carr 1999).

The five main strands of this pedagogical approach for children and families are to feel that they belong in the community of the Early Years setting, to ensure that children's and families' well-being is safeguarded, an exploration of the environment, an emphasis on communication, and, finally, to ensure that individual (and/or group) contributions are valued. Within this framework Carr (2001) emphasises the importance of assessment as a continuous process based on observations. Carr suggests that through assessing children's experiences, Early Years practitioners can look at whether children are:

- taking an interest;

- coping with change and difference;

- connecting places and experiences together;

- finding out new things;

- practising old things;

- tackling difficulty;

- developing relationships with adults;

- developing relationships with peers;

- taking responsibility.

(Carr, 1998, p.15)

Carr (1998) introduces the idea of 'learning dispositions'. Learning dispositions are central in the Te Whaariki curriculum, and are about encouraging children's positive experiences with knowledge, developing the skills and strategies that children will accumulate, and which will help them not only during childhood, but acquiring skills that will be of benefit throughout the rest of their lives. Thus assessment is central to this process, in order for Early Years practitioners to be able to help children in cultivating these dispositions.

It is among the principles of Te Whaariki that children are producing 'working theories' about themselves, and about the people, places and activities in their lives, and that these working theories 'become increasingly useful for making sense of the world, for giving a child control over what happens, for problem solving, and for further learning.' (Te Whaariki, p.44).

What is interesting and important in the Te Whaariki curriculum is the freedom of Early Years settings to create their own programmes given a common framework of principles. Each small community has their own cultures, traditions and needs, and real world experiences can be transformed within the class. A second important aspect of this curriculum is the emphasis on children's interests and needs. In this way, the metaphorical reference made to weaving by Te Whaariki ('woven mat') takes shape. Children's cultural backgrounds, language and interests are an integral part of the Early Years practice.

PRACTICAL TASK

Can you compare these three Early Years curricula? What similarities and differences can you can identify? How can this influence your own practice?

Start this task by identifying how each curriculum views the child, and what developmental theories might underpin each of them.

CHAPTER SUMMARY

This chapter aimed to discuss the influential developmental theories in Early Years, in an attempt to search for some principles for forming a pedagogy for the Early Years. A main emphasis on the ideas of Piaget and Vygotsky, and how these apply to an Early Years class, was presented. In the search for a pedagogical framework for Early Years practice some conditions of learning were identified.

- Emphasis on children's development.

- Emphasis on children's play.

- Emphasis on children's needs.

- Emphasis on children's freedom to choose materials and activities.

- Emphasis on children's ownership of their learning.

There followed an attempt to reflect on the EYFS by drawing examples from international other curriculum practices, such as Reggio Emilia and Te Whaariki.

From the EYFS, and the Reggio Emilia and Te Whaariki approaches we can see that wherever there is formally written or unwritten informal curricula observation appears as the main tool for Early Years practitioners. In some curricula, like EYFS, the monitoring process of children is more formalised in terms of assessment, whilst in others (such as Reggio Emilia or Te Whaariki) it is less formal and less standardised. However, within each curriculum approach to Early Years practice, in order to monitor/assess children's progress, as well as evaluating the education programme itself, there is a need to be observing children. The following chapter will discuss observations in this context.

FURTHER READING

Bruce, T. (2006) *Early childhood: a guide for students*, London: Sage.

Carr, M. (1998) *Assessing children's learning in early childhood settings: a development programme for discussion and reflection*, Wellington: New Zealand Council for Educational Research.

Clark, A. and Moss, P. (2001) *Listening to young children: the Mosaic approach*, London: National Children's Bureau.

MacNaughton, G. (2003) *Shaping early childhood, learners, curriculum and contexts*, Maidenhead: Open University Press.

Smidt, S. (2007) *A guide to early years practice* (3rd edn), London: Routledge.

Rodger, R. (2003) *Planning an appropriate curriculum for the under fives*, (2nd edn), London: David Fulton Publishers.

2 The role of observation in Early Years

CHAPTER OBJECTIVES

By the end of this chapter you should:
- understand the nature of observation within early childhood education and care, and how this is related to Early Years practice;
- be able to relate observations within current policy, and evaluate the extent to which this affects your practice;
- be able to identify and reflect on connections between knowledge and understanding of early childhood education, and on the role of systematic observation within this context.

This chapter addresses the following Standards for EYPS: S10, S12, S21, S24, and S27.

Introduction

This chapter discusses the nature of observations. It begins by raising the questions of, and the reasons why, Early Years practitioners carry out observations. It considers the skills that practitioners should develop as one of the main factors involved when working with young children. It will discuss the importance and challenges of multi-agency work in relation to the government agenda 'Every Child Matters'.

The six aims of the Common Assessment Framework are incorporated within this, and we discuss how a common framework can be developed via observations. This common framework builds upon familiarity with the basic methods necessary in observing children. Many testing instruments and observational methods have been developed, modified and validated by current research. Throughout this chapter you ought to consider how observations are a tool for practitioners to assess and evaluate, in partnership with the parents, a young child's development and learning. Finally, we will explore the imperatives for Early Years Professionals to develop and implement systematic ways of observing young children.

Observation in context

Observations play an important role in the Early Years Foundation Stage (DCSF, 2008a). One of the main principles, outlined within the EYFS, clearly states that observations, assessment and planning are all central points of practice within the Early Years setting. It emphasises that these observations of children should prioritise a child's development and learning. At the same time it stresses the importance of observations in terms of planning activities.

In 1990 The Rumbold Report emphasised the importance of assessment in context:

> We believe there is a need for guidance for educators on the achievement of more consistent and coherent approaches to observing, assessing, recording and reporting children's progress in preschools provision [. . .] such guidance is to inform and to improve on what is offered to the under fives and the early stages of the post five provision. (DfES, The Rumbold Report, 1990, p.17)

Ten years later, one of the key principles identified within the Curriculum Guidance for the Foundation Stage was that: 'practitioners must be able to observe and respond appropriately to children, informed by a knowledge of how children develop and learn' (QCA, 2000, p.11).

Today there are expectations for professionals within Early Years settings to be able to observe, record and assess young children. The Early Years Foundation Stage (DCSF, 2008a), implemented in September 2008, has four main principles.

- an emphasis on the individual child as a learner;
- a recognition of the interpersonal relationships and the loving environment that all children need in order to develop;
- an appreciation of the learning environment as a vehicle for all children's development and learning;
- an identification of children's individual ways of personal development.

As a statutory document, these principles inform the work of all Early Years professionals.

Moreover, since 2007, the graduate Early Years Professional (EYP) role is now a reality. Two of the standards that EYP candidates must be able to meet within their own practice (and also lead and support others in) in order to achieve Early Years Professional Status relate directly to observing children:

- to 'assess, record, and report on progress in children's development and learning, and use this as a basis for differentiating provision' (CWDC, 2006, S21 p.7);
- to 'use close informed observation and other strategies to monitor children's activity, development and progress systematically and carefully, and to use this information to inform, plan and improve upon practice and provision' (S10).

Consequently, as an EYP you need to be aware of the relevance of systematic methods of observation, for gathering evidence of children's behaviour and their interactions with the environment around them. 'The EYFS profile is a good starting point for observing individual children and assessing their developmental needs' (Willan, 2007, p.118).

Although observations, traditionally, have been used by practitioners working in the Early Years sector, the statutory requirements for teaching and assessing young children in the Early Years Foundation Stage (DCSF, 2008a) mean that it is also essential to develop a more systematic approach to observations.

The Early Years workforce is moving towards that of a multidisciplinary and multi-professional one. That means that professionals from different sectors (such as Education, Social Work, Psychology and Health) will work together in order to meet the *Every Child Matters* five outcomes.

- Be healthy.

- Be safe.

- Enjoy and achieve.

- Make positive contribution.

- Achieve economic well-being.

Within *Every Child Matters* is outlined the Common Assessment Framework (CAF) for children and young people: the CAF aims to be used with children who are at risk of failing to meet the five Every Child Matters outcomes (HM Government, 2006b). The Common Assessment Framework (HM Government, 2006b) has been introduced, and it is a requirement that all professionals should be able to communicate and share information effectively about children. It states that 'it is particularly suitable for use in universal services (health, education, etc.), to identify and tackle problems before they become serious'.

The Common Assessment Framework is designed to become a preventative tool in the hands of the Early Years Professional. Throughout the CAF there is an emphasis on the 'common assessment processes' by all key staff working with children, in order to meet children's needs. It also recognises that the CAF aims not only to formalise existing practices in many sectors, but also aims to become the basis for creating a portrait for children, where needs are met and covered, and where early interventions are taking place in a proactive manner. A full common assessment framework includes the collection of information on a child's development. Parents/carers and the family environment are involved in this process. The areas that are covered in a common assessment are as follows.

- Development of the infant child and young person.

- Health.

- development (physical development, speech, language and communication development, emotional and social development, behavioural development, identity (including self esteem), self image, and social presentation);

- family and social relationships;

- self-care skills and independence;

- learning (understanding, reasoning and problem solving, participation in learning, education and employment, progress and achievement in learning, and aspirations);

- safety and protection;

- emotional warmth and stability.

PRACTICAL TASK

Read the Common Assessment Framework for children and young people: practitioners guide *(CWDC, 2007c) pp. 28–34 (You can access this document from the following web page:*

http://www.cwdcouncil.org.uk/pdf/Integrated%20Working/CAF_Practitioners_Guide_Sept 07.pdf)

Reflect on the areas that are covered in a common assessment. Do they offer a good and helpful basis for your work with babies and young children?

The nature of observations

Although there is a wealth of literature about observations, Drummond (1993) suggests that we ought to develop manageable systems for being able to watch children interacting with one another, and their environment, in order to create comprehensive portraits of children as autonomous individuals.

> *. . . Observing learning, [and] getting close to children's minds and children's feelings, is part of our daily work in striving for quality. Our careful observations of children's learning can help us make [Early Years] provision better. We can use what we see to identify the strengths and weaknesses, gaps and inconsistencies, in what we provide. We can identify significant moments in a child's learning, and we can build on what we see. (Drummond, 1998, p.105)*

When considering the nature of observations, the main goal should be to help practitioners to understand development and to help plan their activities and practices, based on children's needs as learners; also, to create an environment where this will 'play a key role in supporting and extending children's development and learning' (DCSF, 2008b, p.5).

When the nature of observations is discussed it is important to understand the term comprehensively. Observation is a method of studying an object or a person within a specific context, and should always have a precise purpose. It involves recording and watching over a period of time. Observations of young children should always have a clear intention. In an attempt to define observations in the Early Years context, we might argue that it is a valid tool for understanding children's development, in order to help Early Years practitioners to assess their development. The term 'observe' literally means 'to look at', to 'watch something closely'. The term 'observation' is used to describe the systematic and 'structured way' (Fargher and MacNaughton, 1998) that Early Years Professionals view children in order to understand them, with the ultimate purpose of assessing their development. This systematic way of scrutinising children enables us to help 'all children achieve their full potential' (EYPS Standard 7) and to 'provide balanced and flexible daily and weekly routines that meet children's needs, and to enable them to develop and learn' (S9, p. 7).

At another level, by observing what children do we understand their development, and the way in which they behave and react within certain situations and contexts. This reflection informs not only our Early Years practice, but is also an important channel of communication for the children's families.

REFLECTIVE TASK

With reference to Early Years Foundation Stage try to answer the following questions.

1 What place do observations have in your setting?

2 How do they inform your practice?

3 How could you use observations to help you learn more about children?

If possible, try to ask the same questions to a more experienced Early Years practitioner in your setting and then compare your answers.

Observations for a reason

Observations are the 'foundation of education in the early years' (Hurst, 1991, p.70). The main reason that observations are part of Early Years practice, and are subsequently emphasised by the EYFS, is that observations can offer us important information about children, their abilities and their interests, that are not available elsewhere. Furthermore, closely watching children via systematic techniques – as will be described in the following chapter – can give the observers and the Early Years Professional an in-depth look at children; this can enhance our understanding of children and their actions. Observations focus on a child's natural behaviour in a given setting, which is the key process for assessing their development. Looking at children closely helps observers to recognise stages of child development, and to take responsibility for helping a child to progress.

Through the systematic collection of information about children, professionals are able to observe incidents and gather evidence, which can then offer an accurate picture about children's behaviours and development. This evidence, gathered through observations, is a very important tool in the hands of professionals, especially in the case of dealing with very young children. Young children have a limited repertoire of language and behaviours, and when professionals are asked to explain and to try to provide a supportive learning environment for young children, first and foremost it is necessary to be able to understand the children involved. Young children, through their play and through their interaction with others, make meaningful suggestions about their thoughts and feelings. Thus, via observations, professionals can collect accurate and pertinent data about these children. Accordingly, the most accurate way for professionals to study children is through these observations.

Systematic observations also help professionals to understand the reasons behind children's behaviour in certain situations. Benjamin (1994) emphasises the importance of the nature of observations: 'Observations play an important role in assessment, either by replacing or by supplementing standardised evaluation instruments' (Benjamin, 1994, p.14).

Consequently, observers can recognise stages of child development, relate these to the stages of development suggested by EYFS (pages 26–116), and then subsequently take responsibility for helping a child's progress. In this sense, observations not only help the Early Years Professional's practice, but also provide a reliable context for professionals to make links between theory and practice, in order to demonstrate what they have learnt about children.

Observations allow theory to be exercised in a practical context and to allow professionals the opportunity to implement theory in their daily practice. It is by no means presumptuous to say that observations facilitate a professional's reflective thinking, and thus empower them to evaluate their own practice in an attempt to develop effectively. Thus there is a dualistic purpose of observations: first and foremost, to help professionals understand children, but also to help professionals to progress within their own practice through reflection.

Observations focus on what a child *can* do (and not on what a child *cannot* do) as a basis for forward planning. It is important to highlight what a child is capable of, in order to plan activities. An observation's main focus is on what children can achieve. Moreover, it is in the nature of observations to focus on a child's natural behaviour within the Early Years setting. The information that is collected can be a valid starting point for assessing a child and his or her development.

Finally, observations offer an in-depth look at a child not available in other ways. Discussion with the parents can offer an insight about their children within the family environment, which is a very helpful tool for professionals – however, there is a necessity for Early Years workers to try and investigate children's behaviour within the context of the classroom.

Luff (2007) stresses another important factor in observing children: 'Observing and documenting learning can be a way of valuing and listening to children' (p.189). Elfer (2005) adds that within current legislations, such as the requirements raised by the Children's Act (HMSO, 2004) and the United Nations Convention on Children's Rights (1989), observations can provide an effective context for listening to children's attempts to communicate, and for professionals to take into consideration a child's distinctive voice.

Thus observations can become a suitable path for opening up communication with children. Evidence through observations helps professionals to consider children's voices, and their needs and experiences, in order to create pedagogical activities that will comply with children's interests. This can create learning environments for children that are not only safe, enjoyable and applicable, but also exciting as well.

It is in the nature of observations to provide opportunities for collaboration. The multi-professional workforce should seek ways of communicating, and sharing information and ideas about their understanding of children, in order to 'promote earlier interventions . . . [and to] improve quality' (HM Government, 2006b). The basis of multi-disciplinary work can be provided by evidence collected via observations '[to] embed a common language about the needs of children' (HM Government, 2006b).

REFLECTIVE TASK

1 *Consider your Early Years setting and try to think of any occasions where observations became a suitable source for listening to children, and what action you subsequently took.*

2 *Can you recall any opportunities where you used information from observations to work in a multi-professional way?*

Here we will argue that observations should be viewed as part of the daily routine of the setting, and not as a separate tool that professionals can use as and when they need it. Observation is *not* a tool where children that have a problem are studied as an attempt to resolve dilemmas. These are instances when there is a specific problem with a child. Observations ought to be implemented during *every day* practice. Observations, as a purposeful tool, should focus on children's development and learning, and an interpretation of observations as a reflection on daily practice '. . . is unobtrusively woven into classroom activity and interaction' (Pratt, 1994, p.102).

Example

An example of how observations have been integrated or 'woven' into the every day life of the classroom comes from New Zealand. As it was discussed in Chapter 1, the curriculum of New Zealand aims to create a multicultural learning environment. 'Te Whaariki' is underpinned by five goals.

• well-being;

• belonging;

• contribution;

• communication;

• exploration.

Consequently, observations look at the behaviours that are central to children. These behaviours are important for the development of children as effective learners. Carr (2001) stresses the importance of children obtaining these behaviours, and thus she suggests the following model of assessment and observation.

Table 2.1 Carr's model of assessment and observation

The strands of the curriculum	The behaviour we look at
Belonging	Taking an interest
Well-being	Being involved
Exploration	Persisting with difficulty, challenges and uncertainty
Communication	Expressing a point of view or feeling
Contribution	Taking responsibility

In Carr's work, as mentioned above, observation is central to the curriculum. It is integrated in the daily practice of the class – 'woven within the curriculum'. It is important to see that observation has a definite purpose, and that this purpose is oriented by curriculum learning objectives and outcomes.

Carr claims that observations are central in creating 'learning communities [. . .] where children [can]:

- take an interest in an activity;

- become involved in it over a sustained period of time;

- persist when they meet difficulty, challenges or uncertainty;

- express their ideas or feelings in a range of ways;

- take responsibility to change the way things are, to teach others, and to listen to another point of view'.

(Carr, 1998, p.15)

According to Carr these processes are linear and they appear in sequence; thus she characterises them as 'Learning Stories'. The main interest and focus on these learning stories is the merging of dispositions, and the accompanying people, places and phenomena that make the emergence more likely, and also of how Early Years practitioners can strengthen these dispositions. The importance of these learning stories is that they provide guidelines for the adults' planning of activities and which, in addition, can also provide families an insight into their children's day and give the parents a view of learning that is valued and encouraged.

So we can see, in the curriculum the use of observation is two-fold; firstly, to help and improve Early Years practitioners' practice, pedagogy and activities, and, secondly, as a valid tool to communicate with the children's families. In addition, the children themselves participate in writing these stories. Therefore observations in the Te Whaariki classroom is part of daily life and routine, and they are not used only in certain circumstances, but as part of the curriculum as a whole, in order to be able to monitor a child's progress.

Carry out an audit of the types of observations that are carried out daily in your setting.

How are these observations integrated within the implementation of EYFS?

Why observe children?

As noted above, observations formalise the link between theory and practice, so professionals are able to demonstrate what they have learned about children across all areas.

Thus far we have discussed what observations should look at. In this section we will briefly discuss what observations should aim towards. To begin with, observations as a methodological tool, in the hands of an Early Years Professional, address a child's development. All aspects of development are under scrutiny where children are involved. Emotional, social, physical, cognitive and moral awareness are all crucial aspects of a child's progress, and these are all interlinked. We might, as Early Years Professionals, study and observe them separately, but they all come together in order to offer us a complete portrait of an individual child's development and progress.

All children go through observable sequences of behaviour at their own pace, and this sequence of development can be traced by the Early Years Professional in the context of them being the observer. The main issue is that the Early Years Professional should know what to look for, and listen to, in each instance.

In the EYFS (pages 26–116) children's development is described in detail. In the 'Look, Listen and Note' section a detailed guideline on each aspect of development is offered to practitioners involved with children. In this section a guideline is also suggested of what Early Years Professionals are to look for when observing young children.

Read the following case study and try to:

- *identify which areas of development Sue needs encouragement in;*
- *use EYFS pages 24–114 as your guideline in order to complete the activity;*
- *consider how can you help Sue and her parents.*

Sue's story

Sue is a two-year-old girl. She is the only child in her family. She has joined the Early Years setting three weeks ago. She is a lively and active child, but she cries a lot every day and the Early Years practitioners cannot calm her. She appears to be in distress, sad and stressed when her mothers leaves her in the morning. She does not interact with other children and she only wants to be in the company of the adults. She does not want to share any toys when she plays and during the activities she sits quietly and does not attempt to communicate with the other children. She does not appear to have made any friends or interactions with other children.

Becoming a skilful observer

As has been demonstrated previously, observations are a purposeful and daily reflective tool for gathering information about children's behaviour, and their needs and development, and this task requires a skilful professional.

One of the key skills that Early Years Professionals should develop is objectivity. This is always a main aspiration that observers should aim for. It is a challenging aspect of the observation, and it does take a lot of practice in order to reach the stage that, as professionals, we try to be objective and record what *actually* happens, and not what we merely *perceive* to be happening. The following activity attempts to demonstrate how difficult it is to be objective and to record what actually does take place.

PRACTICAL TASK

Look at the picture and write down what you see. Then show the picture to a colleague or to a fellow student or EYP candidate, and ask this person to do the same. Now compare your answers. Are they the same? Do you see what it is actually there?

Figure 2.1 Children at the book area

Have you written, 'There are two boys reading books'?

But what do you actually see? You see two boys holding books. Whether these two boys read the books is an interpretation of what is seen.

This is a clear example of one of the main challenges when we observe young children. It is difficult to step out of our personal values, beliefs and cultural stereotypes, and to retain objectivity when we record our observations.

Consequently, the second challenge for the professional is not only to step back from personal values and beliefs, but also to step out of the role that these normally signify. There are times when the systematic observer should not interfere with the activity of the child in question. Within the daily life of the classroom or setting the Early Years Professional is faced with a number of tasks, and when he or she has to deliver activities with the children it is challenging to step out of the 'educator' role and become an observer. This is a constant exercise and it will be discussed more comprehensively in the next chapter.

It is important that when an observation is taking place the observer judges whether the collection of information is 'disturbed'. In such a case the observer needs to stop the observation if the child, or children, is distracted or the observation is unduly distorted, as attention and concentration on the task will be lost.

The challenging task of observation not only requires objectivity – in addition to training to distance yourself from your normal role as a systematic observer – but also to consider that your emotions are involved. As Willan (2007) argues:

> *Both child and observer come with their own load of emotional baggage. The child being observed or assessed has feelings, as do the parents, carers and educators around him/her – and so, of course, does the observer. It is important to be aware of the emotional dimension of the observational context, and to try to take it into account as part of the assessment process. (p.109)*

The process of observation takes place in the natural environment of the child and the Early Years setting where children stay for a great amount of their day. Within this context there are a number of pressures for the Early Years Professional. There is always the pressure for children to be safe, for them to be able to participate and enjoy activities, and there is also the additional pressure of being capable of observing objectively without bringing any values, beliefs or stereotypes into the process.

In this context the observer should participate as emotionally 'unbiased' towards the child observed. However, it is difficult to achieve such an emotionally unbiased equilibrium whilst you observe a child.

Luff (2007) adds to this point, and elaborates upon another difficulty:

> *The processes for learning using documentation are, therefore, highly complex. An additional challenge for English Early Years Professionals is a requirement to work in two*

potentially contradictory ways. On the one hand, observations can create opportunities to plan according to carefully looking at, and listening to, children's actions and responses; on the other hand, Early Years Professionals are expected to work towards specific pre-set learning outcomes. As skilled professionals, Early Years practitioners must therefore gain confidence in demonstrating how specified criteria can be met through flexible holistic ways of working, [and] also need to find means of using structured guidelines, such as the EYFS, as frameworks for their observations. (p.187)

In addition to these skills, there is also a need to involve parents in the observation of their children. As mentioned earlier, observations can become a valid path of communication between Early Years Professionals and the children's families. Parental involvement is important in the process of observations and assessments of their children. By involving the parents it is felt that they participate in the life of their children whilst they are in the Early Years setting. Moreover, parents feel more comfortable about their child's daily life in the classroom, and this subsequently minimises the risk of feeling inordinately judged by the Early Years environment. Asking for parents' help might assist Early Years professionals to achieve 'emotionally unbiased' skills, and to offer a more in-depth insight into the aspects of the children's behaviour, and subsequently into the development that is under scrutiny.

As well as involving the parents, it is essential the children can also be heard within this process. Daily observations in the Early Years environment offer opportunities for listening to children's own voices. Clark and Moss (2001) carried out a study aiming to search '. . . for a way to listen to young children [talk] about their lives' (p.11), and demonstrates the effects of listening to children, and also suggests ways of implementing ways of taking into consideration children's voices, experiences and interests.

As a result, they developed the Mosaic approach, which is a way of not only listening to children's distinct voices (a requirement of the EYFS, Children's Act and the United Nations Convention on Children's Rights, as mentioned earlier), but also children's views are respected in an empowering way. Clark and Moss (2001) describe three fundamental conditions for empowering children's voices, when we create an environment where there are going to be conditions for listening to children.

Firstly, they introduce a 'climate of listening' whereby children's experiences, interests and views influence their relationship to adults and to their environment; secondly, they stress the importance of allowing time to listen to children. 'The Mosaic approach involves a time of communication for Early Years staff in several ways.

- Gathering the material will take longer because we are not relying on a single method of communication.
- Interpreting the material gathered is time consuming' (p. 64).

Thirdly, they also emphasise the significant place of staff training, not only in order to listen to children, but, in addition, training in terms of understanding children's development, and the ways in which children make attempts to communicate, learn and obtain the skills that they will use throughout their lives.

The process of becoming a skilful observer is complex and challenging. It requires constant self-development, self-assessment, an addressing of individual needs, and the overcoming of personal emotional boundaries.

PRACTICAL TASK

- *Read the following extract and try to identify the main skills that Early Years Professionals should develop in order to become competent observers.*

- *Which of these skills do you feel you already have?*

Hamilton, C., Haywood, S., Gibbins, S., McInnes, K., and Williams, J. (2003) Principles and practice in the foundation stage, *Learning Matters (p.61)*

One of the greatest challenges is the need to be objective and unbiased. We must not allow objectivity to be influenced by preconceived ideas about the child's attainment.

Observation can also be a time consuming process. It does need to be carefully organised and managed within the setting or classroom, so that everyone is aware of their role and responsibility, in relation to observation and assessment. It is essential to involve all those working with children in the observation and assessment process, and this needs careful organisation, management and training for all those who are going to be carrying out these processes. Devising ways of integrating observation into practice within a reception class, particularly if there are no additional adults working with you, requires creativity and a commitment to the value of this as an essential tool for your professional practice. Observation can also be professionally demanding for practitioners. These demands can take the form of being surprised or threatened by the information gathered through observation. When gathering observation data it is also likely that one will be observing the adults working with children more carefully than usual, and this may also engender a sense of fear and anxiety within the adults. A final challenge to practitioners is that of interpreting or analysing the information that has been gathered. You need to use your understanding of child development, along with your professional knowledge, to interpret what you see and hear and take the child's learning forward or change your own practice. This is often best achieved though discussions with all those involved in the setting, including nursery nurses, teaching assistants, key workers and other practitioners. A key factor in this process of interpretation is ensuring that the evidence you are working with is gathered objectively, and accurately taking account of the challenges that are identified above.

C H A P T E R   S U M M A R Y

This chapter has investigated the nature of observations within the contemporary Early Years setting. In the light of the current Government policies regarding the Early Years, these observations hold an important and essential role. Here are the key points of discussion in each section.

Observation in context

- There is a need for a systematic way of making observations within the Early Years.

- Observations are the structured way of studying children.

- Observations should inform pedagogy and curriculum structure, and should also underpin the everyday activities of the classroom.

- Observations can become the basis for multi-professional collaboration.

Observations for a reason

- To find out about children as individuals.

- To monitor their progress.

- To inform curriculum planning.

- To enable staff to evaluate the provisions that they make.

- To provide a focus for discussion and improvement.

- To understand Early Years practice better.

- Observations are 'woven' into Early Years daily practice.

Observations look at

- emotional development;

- social development;

- physical development;

- cognitive development;

- language;

- creative abilities;

- literacy and numeracy.

Becoming a skilful observer

- To become a systematic observer of children you need to develop objectivity and absence of emotional bias, and you must therefore first step out of the role that you normally hold.

- Parental involvement, child involvement, and confidentiality are essential skills towards a systematic way of observing children.

The next chapter attempts to discuss the variety of observation techniques that are available to the professional.

Carr, M. (2001) *Assessment in early childhood settings*, London: Paul Chapman Publishing.

Drummond, M.J. (2003) *Assessing children's learning*, 2nd edn, London: David Fulton.

Drummond, M.J. (1998) Observing children, in S. Smidt (ed.) *The early years: a reader*, London: Routledge.

Useful websites

http://www.everychildmatters.gov.uk/deliveringservices/caf/

3 Observation techniques

Introduction

The Statutory Framework for the EYFS (DCSF, 2008a, p.16) asserts that

> *ongoing assessment is an integral part of the learning and development process. Providers must ensure that practitioners are observing children and responding appropriately to help them make progress from birth towards the early learning goals. Assessments should be based on practitioners' observations of what children are doing in their day to day activities.*

It is also stated that all the evidence for children's assessment should have been gathered by observational recordings. Within this requirement there is a necessity for the Early Years Professional to be aware of the variety of observation techniques. This chapter aims to explore the observation techniques that there are to facilitate the work of professionals involved with children.

As was explained in Chapter 2, observations should always have a purpose. For the Early Years Professional working with the EYFS this purpose is clearly stated. The general and ultimate goal of observations is to collect information to give as complete a picture as possible of the child for assessment purposes. However, in this chapter it will be stressed that observations can have an important secondary aim of collecting information to enable practitioners to evaluate their own educational programmes, activities and curriculum, and through this systematic evidence inform future planning.

Observation techniques

There are two types of observations that Early Years Professionals can use. These are participant and non-participant observations. The following paragraphs describe these techniques and offer an evaluation of them.

Participant observation

As it is part of the daily routine, participant observation is well known within the Early Years profession. When Early Years Professionals work with children they either record an event that occurs by writing down quick notes at the time of the event, or later, after the event. These brief and immediate notes that Early Years Professionals use are part of an ongoing daily practice. The event is recorded when the professional is working with the children directly and the professional does not withdraw himself or herself from the children in order to observe. These recordings are usually brief comments about a child's behaviour during an activity, or are comments on how the activity was implemented.

There are a number of advantages when the professionals are using participant observation. Daily events that they record can provide the practitioner with a useful insight into a child or an activity. Special training is not required, as the professional writes down their perception of an event as it occurs. This type of observation is unstructured and the observer writes down what appears to them to be most interesting and relevant at the time. It does not require planning or organisation, and it is useful as the observer records events such as unexpected behaviour or an unexpected change within an activity.

However, there are obvious limitations to this type of observation. This type of observation will not give a complete picture of the events that occur and require the professional to rely on memory, as events will be largely recorded after they have happened.

As Devereux (2003) points out, participant observation can be messy and difficult to manage and it should be categorised and filed immediately, otherwise useful evidence could be lost. An additional disadvantage to this type of observation technique is that the recorded information could be examined long after an event, thus allowing the potential for an inaccurate and biased interpretation of events.

However, despite the disadvantages of using participant observation, it is a very simple and immediate tool to use in collecting information as events occur, and can be used to capture unexpected events during the day.

REFLECTIVE TASK

Can you list any further disadvantages of participant observation?

There are ways to help limit the disadvantages of this type of observation. Professionals can have pre-prepared forms to record occurrences quickly. The following information can be included.

✓ Name of the observer.

✓ Name of the child.

✓ Date of observation.

✓ Starting time.

✓ Finishing time.

✓ Number of adults present.

✓ Area of observation.

✓ Description of the activity observed.

✓ Additional comments.

This obviously speeds up the recording process, facilitates the filing of recordings and when you return to the observation all the information will be included, which makes retrieval and interpretation much easier.

CASE STUDY

Kenzie is four years and eleven months. Recently his attendance has become very erratic with absences noted at the beginning and end of weeks. The aim of the observation is to identify whether these frequent absences are affecting his ability to make and sustain friendships.

Aim: to look for evidence of social play and participation

Observation 1

Name of the observer: *Emily (EYP)*
Name of the child: *Kenzie, 4 years and 11 months*
Date of observation: *9/11/07*
Starting time: *10:30*
Finishing time: *10:34*
No. of adults present: *1 adult*
Area of observation: *free play outdoors*

Description of the activity observed
It is an outdoor play time and Kenzie is in the corner of the playground kicking leaves that have fallen from a tree. He is on his own, smiling and his arms are waving freely as he kicks the leaves. Liam, who has been playing with a group of three other boys approaches Kenzie and says 'Come play' It's me Jack and Tommy'. Kenzie drops his head, looking towards the floor and his arms and legs remain still whilst Liam is speaking to him. Liam returns to his group of friends without Kenzie who continues to droop his head and to remain motionless.

Additional comment

Prior to Kenzie being approached by his peer, he was involved in play. Kenzie appeared to be joyfully content with solitary play and there was a definite change to his body language when Liam joined him. This event seems to support the concerns raised as Kenzie refused to answer Liam and also preferred not to make any eye contact.

Observation 2

Name of the observer:	Emily (EYP)
Name of the child:	Kenzie, 4 years and 11 months
Date of observation:	9/11/07
Starting time:	11:40
Finishing time:	11:45
No. of adults present:	1 adult
Area of observation:	writing area

Description of the activity observed

Kenzie is sitting at a table with three other children. There is a tub of wax crayons close to him on the table and he has a picture of a lollipop lady in front of him that he has been asked to colour in. He is looking down at his lollipop lady picture and his tongue is moving from side to side as he holds a red wax crayon to the paper. Toby says to Kenzie: 'I need a green, can I have a green crayon?' Kenzie remains silent and lifts his head to face Toby. Kenzie reaches out his left arm towards the tub of crayons, scoops the tub in the crook of his arm and pulls it towards his body. His eyebrows are lowered and his lips are puckered tightly.

Additional comments

Kenzie is choosing not to communicate with Toby. He is capable of expressing himself and could well have asked Toby to wait until he had finished with the green crayon and put it back into the tub or give it to Toby. He does not want to share (something that he did earlier in the sand area as well). He makes eye contact on this occasion.

Observation 3

Name of the observer:	Emily (EYP)
Name of the child:	Kenzie, 4 years and 11 months
Date of observation:	11/11/07
Starting time:	10:15
Finishing time:	11:20
No. of adults present:	1 adult
Area of observation:	outdoors play

CASE STUDY continued

Description of the activity observed

During outdoor free play, Kenzie is sitting on a tricycle. He is pedalling, raising his head and 'La-La-ing' a tune loudly. Tommy and Claire run over to Kenzie, and Tommy shouts excitedly, 'We are playing trains! Come make a big, long train.'

Kenzie stops pedalling and quietens whilst Tommy is talking. Kenzie is looking and smiling at Tommy and he is getting off the tricycle. Both of his arms are up in the air and he is shouting, 'Yeah, big train, yeah!' The three children run off together and form a line by standing one behind the other. They are all running around in a line, laughing and making: 'Woo-hoo' noises.

Additional comments

Since the last observations it appears that there is a progress in terms of making friendships. Other member of staff report that he seems to have settled in well and engages actively in most activities. He spends a lot of free play with Tommy. He has even started to bring items to the 'Show and Tell' time at the beginning of the morning session, which also demonstrates a big social step forward.

PRACTICAL TASK

In your Early Years setting undertake at least three participant observations. Share your observations with a more experienced colleague or a fellow student. Was it difficult to find time to observe events and, if so, how did you overcome this?

Remember to:

- *be factual and objective;*

- *record when and where it happened;*

- *record what was said and done;*

- *record facial expressions, body language, tones of voices, gestures.*

Non-participant observation

This type of observation is a systematic observation and requires a number of techniques as described below. Non-participant observation requires the professional to step outside the role of practitioner, and not to be involved in interacting with the children, acting instead as an objective observer of the child or an activity.

Preparation and organisation is required for non-participant observation and it needs to be planned in advance. It is statutory within the EYFS to provide a profile in the form of a portfolio for each child at the end of the EYFS: 'The EYPS Profile is a way of summing up each child's development and learning achievements at the end of the EYFS. It is based on practitioners' ongoing observations and assessments in all six areas of Learning and Development' (DCSF, 2008a, p.16).

For the Early Years Professional to be able to meet the requirements of the EYFS and be able to complete the assessment scales described in the EYFS Statutory Framework (DCSF, 2008a, pp. 44–48), a systematic preparation towards this type of observations is crucial.

Preparing observations

When the Early Years team is planning how individual children's profiles will be built and when developing strategies for evaluating the educational programme and its activities, observations are the tool for collecting this evidence. It is important that members of the Early Years team share roles and responsibilities before they start, and clarify and set aims and objectives for the observations. This way the team will remain focused and collect rich evidence to effectively complete each child's profile, and also to evaluate the education programme itself.

Objectives for undertaking the observations should be clearly defined, as the objectives will determine the nature of the information to be gathered. According to Riddall-Leech (2005) 'Objectives should give a detailed reason for the observation, be achievable and measurable, be underpinned, either by developmental milestones or norms or in another acceptable way such as theory or theoretical perspectives'.

Within the EYFS the learning goals need to be met but due to the broad nature of the six learning areas it is important to set clear objectives. These will enable the gathering of comprehensive evidence around each goal. Clear aims and objectives will also allow you to choose the most appropriate observation technique. As inclusive practitioners, aims and objectives ought to be shared with the parents and carers of children, and be modified in the light of subsequent comments that might be made.

The EYP as lead practitioner should involve the whole team in the process of agreeing who will carry out the observations, and also ensure that all team members gain the valuable experience of undertaking observations.

Clear roles within the Early Years setting should be decided upon, so that the practitioner undertaking the observation knows when to remove themselves from activities in preparation to observe. It is also important that children know in advance who is the observer in that activity although, of course, with very young children this cannot always achieved. Chapter 4 will elaborate further on this.

Preparing for the role of the observer

To become a systematic observer of children, you must first step out of the role you normally hold. Once you have decided when your observations will take place you must withdraw yourself from your role in the room and take the role of the systematic observer instead. You should position yourself close to what you want to observe, but not interfere with the focus child/children or activity you are observing. Your presence as an observer should be discreet. You must not announce to the children that you are doing an observation and the children should be left alone. Sit closely, however, so that you can see and hear what happens. However, if a child interrupts your observation it is better to stop the observation, rather than gather patchy and inaccurate information.

The best time to undertake observations will be determined by the aims and objectives of the observation. For example, an investigation of activities that are popular with children on arrival will be conducted, appropriately, at arrival time. If you wish to observe children's language development this could be done through a variety of observations at different times of the day.

Similarly, the type of activity to be observed should be related to your aims and objectives. You may, for example, wish to investigate the social interactions of a child during story time.

However, there will be cases where the type of activity to be observed is not always implicit in your aims and objectives. For example, your aim could be to observe social skills and your objective is to investigate whether the focus child 'forms good relationships with peers'. In these instances it is important to refer back to the initial team meetings and reconsider the planning notes.

As discussed in the participant observation section, it is helpful to have forms already prepared. Again, these will include:

✓ name of the observer;

✓ name of the child;

✓ date of observation;

✓ starting time;

✓ finishing time;

✓ no. of adults present;

✓ area of observation;

✓ description of the activity observed;

✓ additional comments.

It is helpful to add comments immediately after the observation has been completed, but care should be taken not to include any of your own comments on the observation itself. It is worth reiterating that observations should only include what *actually* occurs. Initial thoughts about what has been observed will give a good basis for later interpretation and analysis.

PRACTICAL TASK

Look at the following photographs and write down what you have observed.

Share your recordings with a fellow student or a more experienced colleague. Have you recorded the same information?

Figure 3.1 Children drawing

Figure 3.2 Children playing

Preparation of the observations is crucial as it speeds up this process. The systematic way of recording your observations will become effective as you categorise, file, retrieve and then analyse your observations.

The observation techniques are explained in the following sections and include an evaluation of each technique.

Written observations, or narratives

This is the most common observation technique used by Early Years Professionals and practitioners. It is a written record of an event as it occurs. The usual process is for the observer to remove themselves from the activity, and observe from a discreet position, avoiding interacting or interrupting the children or the activities. Each observation is brief (no more than five minutes) and requires accurately recording exactly what happens at the time. These are written in the present tense. Pre-prepared forms are used for this. An example is given in the case study below.

CASE STUDY

Name of child/children: Vicky

No. of adults present: 1

No. of children present: 2

Activity: cooking

Area: writing area

Date of observation: 4/07/07

Starting time of observation: 13:45

Finishing time of observation: 13:50

Aim: social development

Objective: to play alongside others

Observation:
Two children and the Early Years Professional (Vicky and Zara, and Maria) are in the writing area and they write down a recipe on a sheet of poster paper.

Maria: So, we need one glass of olive oil, and do you remember what else we wrote?

Zara: Sugar?

Maria: Can you remember how many glasses of sugar we need?

Vicky: Three, and four glasses of that . . . (she points to the water).

Maria: (pointing to the word 'water') Here, it says 'water'. We need four glasses of water.

Maria: What else did we say?

Vicky: Two glasses of that.

Maria: What is it?

Vicky: I don't know

Zara: Is this semolina?

Vicky: . . . semolina.

Maria: And how many glasses of semolina do we need?

Vicky: . . . two?

Zara: Where does this say 'two'?

Vicky: (points to the poster) Here.

Maria: Yes. If you look here, we need two glasses of semolina.

Comment: (a brief comment may be added here)

The children were working together with Maria in order to make sense of the recipe. Zara was helping Vicky, and with the help of the practitioner they were trying to cook. The children show some evidence of working together towards a common purpose.

Evaluation

As this is an unstructured observation, the observer records anything and everything that happens (such as dialogues, movements, emotions) and this offers rich evidence of the children's behaviours or the implementation of activities. Among the advantages of this technique, the recordings are:

- accurate;
- complete;
- comprehensive.

However, as the observer records what happens at the time, the information recorded can be taken out of context and is open to biased and inaccurate interpretations. A further disadvantage is that the observer may have omitted some relevant information that would therefore present an incomplete and patchy picture of the event. In a busy environment where the observer is an integral part of the team, it may not always be possible or practical to release the team member in order to undertake an uninterrupted observation.

PRACTICAL TASK

In your Early Years setting undertake at least three written observations. Set clear aims and objectives for undertaking these observations. Be clear with yourself at what point of the day you anticipate undertaking the observations.

Evaluate the process, namely:

- *Have I included all the relevant information and details?*

- *Have I included any judgements or comments?*

- *Could I have missed significant events?*

Checklists

Checklists are a very useful observation technique. It is a relatively difficult technique compared to narratives, as careful planning and preparation is required. Checklists can be used to record the activities of a single child or a group of children. They can also be used to record the progress of an activity for evaluation purposes. They are a useful tool for the Early Years Professional, offering specific information and providing a starting point for planning activities for individuals or for groups of children.

The EYFS assessment scales provide a helpful starting point in creating a checklist.

Designing a checklist is not an easy task. The following are things to keep in mind when you create a checklist.

- Length of checklists – keep them short.

- Include items that are representative to the behaviour that you are focusing on.

- Include items that are representative of the age of the children you are observing.

- Ensure that they can be understood by the whole team.

The EYFS learning goals encompass all areas of development:

- personal, social and emotional development;

- communication, language and literacy;

- problem solving, reasoning and numeracy;

- knowledge and understanding of the world;

- physical development;

- creative development.

These learning goals are set as thirteen assessment scales, each of which have nine points. However, these points are too broad to be replicated simply as a checklist. For example, look at the communication, language and literacy section.

Communication, language and literacy

Language for communication and thinking

1 *Listens and responds.*

2 *Initiates communication with others, displaying greater confidence in more informal contexts.*

3 *Talks activities through, reflecting on and modifying actions.*

4 *Listens with enjoyment to stories, songs, rhymes and poems, sustains attentive listening and responds with relevant comments, questions or actions.*

5 *Uses language to imagine and recreate roles and experiences.*

6 *Interacts with others in a variety of contexts, negotiating plans and activities and taking turns in conversation.*

7 *Uses talk to organise, sequence and clarify thinking, ideas, feelings and events, exploring the meanings and sounds of new words.*

8 *Speaks clearly and with confidence and control, showing awareness of the listener.*

9 *Talks, listens confidently and with control, consistently showing awareness of the listener by including relevant detail. Uses language to work out and clarify ideas, showing control of a range of appropriate vocabulary (DCSF, 2008a, p.45)*

The EYP is required to collect information around each of these areas to create a profile for each child. Focusing on the assessment scale above, this cannot stand as an independent comprehensive checklist, and should not be used as such so it needs to be developed further. Focusing on point 1 –'Listens and responds'– you need to collect evidence that demonstrates that the child can listen and respond within different activities across a sustained period of time. 'Listens and responds' can be broken down into 'when' and 'how'.

PRACTICAL TASK

Look at the checklist below, which attempts to record a child's behaviour during storytelling time.

- *Which of the items below capture listening behaviours?*

- *Are there any additional items to be added to the list?*

- *In what ways is this a useful tool for the EYP?*

Name of Child:	*Ian*
Date:	*8/09/2007*
No. of adults present:	*1*
No. of children present:	*2*
Activity:	*story time*
Area:	*carpet*
Aim:	*language development*

PRACTICAL TASK *continued*

Objective: listens and responds

1 Looks at teacher directly

2 Child pays attention

3 Facial movements

   3a) Smile

   3b) Impressed

   3c) Apathetic

4 Uses body language

   4a) Movement

   4b) Direction

   4c) Emotion

   4d) Relaxation

   4e) Interest

5 Asks questions

6 Joins in discussion

7 Answers questions

8 Predicts events from the book

PRACTICAL TASK

Using the EYFS learning goals as your guide, create a checklist for social development. How are you going to tackle in your checklist the objective 'works as part of a group or class by taking turns and showing sharing fairly'. Consider the timing of your observation and specific items to include in your checklist.

Evaluation

Observation checklists can be quick, easy and efficient tools if the checklist is carefully constructed. Checklists can be reused and adapted – gaps in the checklist may be identified, children may demonstrate unanticipated behaviour, or the setting may have particular needs to be incorporated into the checklist. Observation checklists can be used discreetly when the child is present. A number of different observers can use the same checklist to ensure that the information gathered is consistent, accurate and reliable.

However, no checklists will be comprehensive and they should always be subject to additions and modifications.

A major disadvantage of using a checklist is that an important piece of information about a child or an activity may not have been included in the checklist. Although checklists provide a breadth of information, they may lack depth of detail. It may be best to use checklists in conjunction with other techniques, to ensure that enough information is collected.

Diagrammatic

This is a focused and purpose-specific observation technique and it includes a number of different methods:

- tracking;
- the use of sociograms;
- the use of histograms;
- the use of bar charts and pie charts.

Tracking

Tracking is used to record the amount of time a child spends on an activity of their choice or an activity that they have been asked to undertake. It does not explain *why* a child spends time on an activity or what a child did – it focuses only on time.

It is a useful tool when you want to observe:

- children's attention;
- and to investigate the play areas preferred by children;
- how many times children visit an area;
- and to keep track of the use of different areas within the classroom.

Tracking can offer quantitative evidence of the above. However, it does not help you to explain why a particular behaviour has occurred. For example, you may want to observe the physical development of children, so you can use tracking to investigate whether children are active during the day. You can track where they go (e.g. tunnel area, play ground, etc.).

You are planning to change the learning areas of your environment. You want to investigate which areas are the most popular among the children during free play so that you can enrich these. Areas that are not used by the children can subsequently be removed or replaced. You plan to carry out observations for one week and you are going to use tracking to do this. You carry out tracking for one week. After completion the observation findings show that the Lego area was the least popular among the children, and so you decide to alter this area and enrich it with other construction materials instead.

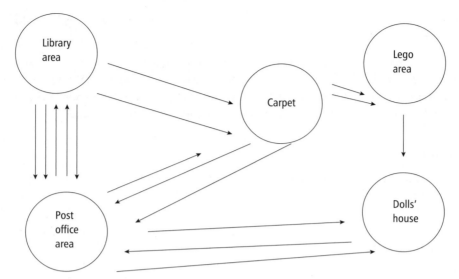

Figure 3.3 Diagram of tracking technique

Sociogram

The focus of this technique is social development. It is a helpful tool to investigate how children interact with others during the day. It investigates the child's relationships with other children or adults and can demonstrate the child's popularity with other children. The main advantage of this technique is that it speeds up the process of observing social development. However, in the same way as tracking, it does not explain the reasons *why* something happens, and can only tell us *what* happens. Sociograms can also offer misleading information as children's relationships can rapidly change.

Example
The aim of the observation is point 5: 'Forms good relationships with adults and peers'. The specific objective is to investigate which children have formed smaller groups of friendships within the bigger class group. You show children three pictures: a smiley face, a sad face and a neutral face. The children are then asked to choose a picture that describes how they feel when they play with other children.

Table 3.1 Examples of the sociogram technique

Group of Children	Gregory	Alison	Gren	Raj
John	☺	😐	☺	☹
Katie	😐	☺	😐	☺
Mathew	☺	☹	😐	☺
Eric	😐	☺	☺	☺
George	☹	😐	😐	😐
Ahmed	☺	☺	☺	😐
Alia	☺	☹	☹	☹

Histograms

Histograms are a helpful technique to follow the development of a child for a long period of time. Histograms are a special form of bar chart where the gathered information is represented continuously rather than in discrete categories. This means that in a histogram there are not gaps between the columns representing the different categories. The main advantage of histograms is that you focus on a child's particular behaviour for a long period of time. As you are able to see the child's behaviour for a long period of time, the gathered information offers an accurate profile of a child.

CASE STUDY

Alia, aged 2 years and 3 months has been finding it difficult to adapt to life in her Early Years setting. A month after joining she keeps crying every day and asks for her mother. The Early Years practitioners have decided to observe her over a period of time to investigate the particular times that she cries the most.

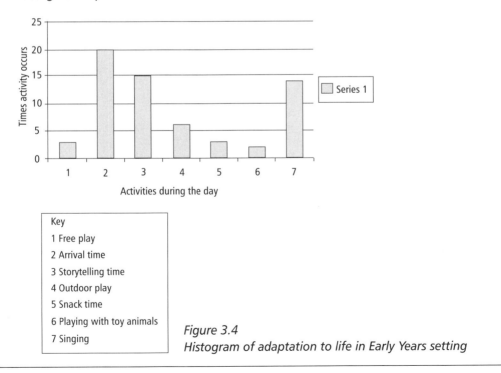

Key

1 Free play

2 Arrival time

3 Storytelling time

4 Outdoor play

5 Snack time

6 Playing with toy animals

7 Singing

Figure 3.4
Histogram of adaptation to life in Early Years setting

Bar charts and pie charts

These can be useful as techniques for collecting information about both groups of children and individual children. They can be produced to offer a visual presentation of the results from your observation recording – 'how children come to the Early Years setting?' for example. Others might include what children eat in a nursery, which areas boys prefer using during the day, which areas girls prefer during the day, or what boys do during outdoor play.

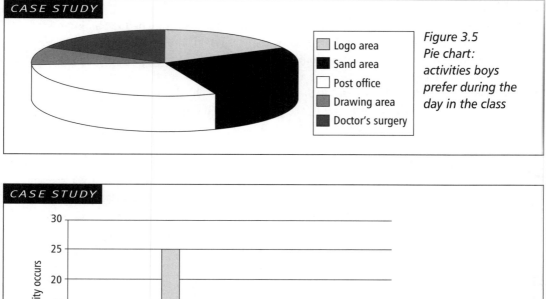

CASE STUDY

- ☐ Logo area
- ■ Sand area
- ☐ Post office
- ■ Drawing area
- ■ Doctor's surgery

Figure 3.5
Pie chart:
activities boys
prefer during the
day in the class

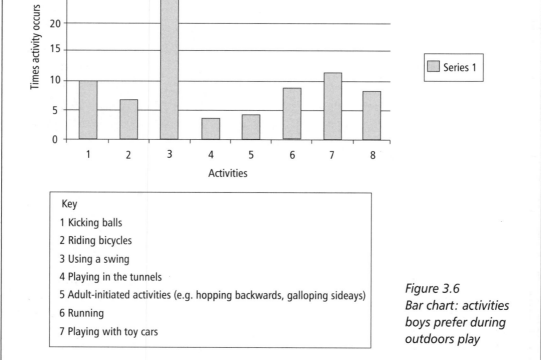

CASE STUDY

Series 1

Key

1 Kicking balls

2 Riding bicycles

3 Using a swing

4 Playing in the tunnels

5 Adult-initiated activities (e.g. hopping backwards, galloping sideays)

6 Running

7 Playing with toy cars

Figure 3.6
Bar chart: activities
boys prefer during
outdoors play

Sampling

The aim of sampling is to identify how and when a particular type of behaviour occurs. Through sampling the emphasis is on the duration of a particular behaviour. For example, you may want to investigate how long a two-and-a-half-year-old child pays attention and focuses on storytelling, or how often a three-year-old visits the sand area.

Time sampling: the observer records whether or not certain behaviours occur over a period of time. The focus of time sampling is on the duration in which particular behaviours occur. As time sampling records behaviours over a period time, the behaviour is shown to be frequent.

The main advantages of time sampling are:

- It takes less time and effort than other techniques.

- It helps you to remain objective as you know the behaviour that you are looking for.

- You can collect data on a number of children or a number for behaviours at the same time, and it provides information at intervals throughout a given period of time.

- It shows the frequencies of behaviour.

However, it is not open-ended. You may miss important behaviours as you are merely recording their frequency and not actually describing the behaviour. Time sampling is thus limited to observable behaviours that occur frequently. This usually focuses on a type of behaviour, and may therefore give a biased view of the behaviour of a child.

CASE STUDY

There are concerns that Val demonstrates some aggressive behaviour. The Early Years practitioners have decided to observe her, in order to find out how frequently Val demonstrates inappropriate behaviours that caused some distress among other children.

In preparing for the time sampling, it is important to define what inappropriate behaviour is. So the EYP, with reference to the EYFS, highlights some specific behaviours that can be easily observed and measurable

1 Turn-taking.

2 Taking toys from other children before they finish with them.

3 Hitting other children.

4 Pushing other children.

5 Shouting at other children.

To make the process faster you can provide a key to your chosen items. For example, you can use numbers, or you can use the first letter of each item. It is up to you to decide how best you are going to code your items. Then you will need to decide when to record these items – for example, departure time, outdoors play, literacy activities, etc. The emphasis on this observation is to record when Val demonstrates inappropriate behaviour.

Table 3.2 Example of time sampling technique

Activity	Time	Behaviour that occurs
Departure time	8:45 a.m.	1 4 5
	9:15 a.m.	2 3
Outdoors play	11:15 a.m.	5 5 4 3 3
	2:20 p.m.	3 1
Storytelling	10:30 a.m.	1 3
Drawing area	3:00 p.m.	3 5 4 2 2
Dancing activity	11:45 a.m.	4 4 4 4 4 5

Key

1. Turn taking
2. Taking toys from other children before they finish with them
3. Hitting other children
4. Pushing other children
5. Shouting at other children

Event sampling

The observer records a specific pre-selected behaviour. Event sampling is used to study the conditions under which particular behaviours occur. It may be important to learn what triggers a particular kind of behaviour, e.g. biting.

Event sampling helps you to keep the event of the behaviour intact. This can make analysis easier and is objective, as behaviour can be defined ahead of time. It is also helpful to record infrequent behaviours. However, it can take the event out of context and, as it looks at specific behaviours, it can be lacking in detail.

Table 3.3 Example of event sampling technique

Behaviours	Departure time	Outdoors play	Storytelling time	Gardening activities
Turn taking	**	*		*****
Hits other children	****	********	****	***
Pushes other children	*******	*****	*******	**
Shouts at other children	*	****		*

Event sampling can help you to investigate what behaviours occur during different times of the day, and with time sampling it is possible to determine how many times that occurs. In this way you can develop strategies to either encourage certain behaviours or discourage others.

Media techniques

With a variety of accessible electronic media now widely available, the Early Years team can use a number of media techniques to improve on and further the observation process. The digital camera or the digital video recorder can be used to add another dimension to the observations. The photographic evidence or tape/video recording evidence cannot replace the traditional observation techniques such as narratives, checklist sampling and diagrammatic methods, but they can be used as additional tools to the observation process. They offer accurate information about events as they capture everything objectively. The Mosaic approach mentioned in Chapter 2, provides an excellent example of how media techniques were used as a useful observation technique to gather information about children's progress through the activities. In the Mosaic approach it was demonstrated how media techniques became a powerful tool to encourage children's participation in contributing to collecting data. They adopted media techniques as 'participatory techniques' for use with children to enable them to be actively involved in the observation process (Clark and Moss, 2001).

PRACTICAL TASK

Try to evaluate the different observation techniques. Your evaluations should aim to answer the following questions.

1 Does this observation technique help me to gain rich information in order to investigate/ answer my specific observation aim/focus/objective?

2 What are the advantages of using this technique? (They always need to be linked with your observation aim/objective/focus.)

3 What are the disadvantages in using this technique? (Again, they must be linked with your observation aim/objective/focus.)

Analysing observation recording

After information has been collected there is a need to analyse the findings. This is a process where all the team needs to get involved and participate. All the data from the observations will be processed during analysis, in order to have a complete picture of either the child under focus or of the education programme.

Analysis is a very difficult part of the process. It requires objectivity and careful consideration of all the facts, in order to offer an accurate portrait for each child and an accurate evaluation of the educational programme.

In order to interpret your observation, and whilst examining the collection of information, it is important that observation recordings are read thoroughly. The next step is to investigate whether there is any interpretation that can be applied to the specific event that you have recorded. Early Years Professionals and practitioners are busy people. They have to look after the children and implement the EYFS, and so during the hectic pace and workload of the day they may have collected data without attempting any interpretation of the incidents collected. In this case an interpretation should be based on valid explanations of the events.

A valid explanation is the one where it can be possible to reach a conclusion derived from the behaviour that you have recorded in your observations. These explanations should not be biased and should not be derived from personal opinions.

CASE STUDY

Observation recording: Vicky would not let Kelly borrow her orange pencil.

A valid and accurate explanation may be the one that says:

Vicky had not finished using her pencil and so she did not give it to Kelly.

A biased explanation may be the one that says:

Vicky does not know how to share.

In this example we do not have enough evidence to support whether Vicky wanted to share or not, and so making such an interpretation would be based on our personal knowledge of Vicky as a child, and not from the recorded observation recordings.

It is easy to draw an inappropriate conclusion on the basis of the evidence. During the observation process, observers must take immediate decisions about what to record. If they do not the results may be superficial or become unreliable as there is no chance of an exact repeat of the behaviour. Often wrong conclusions can also be made when information about prior activities cannot be obtained. Therefore, it is helpful for observations to be repeated either by another person or at different times during the day or on different days so that reliability can be checked.

Observations can provide highly accurate, detailed and verifiable information (Moore, 2001). However, as mentioned in Chapter 2, they are susceptible to bias, which occurs either because of the observer's lack of attention to significant events, or the observer records something they thought they saw rather than what did actually occur (Simpson, et. al, 1995). So the final step in the process of analysing observation recordings is how you arrive at conclusions. Conclusions should be based on a number of valid and accurate explanations of the observation recordings. In these conclusions you need more evidence to back up your final statement. Conclusions are judgements that are made from a number of valid explanations of observation recordings and observation evidence. For example, in the above case if we had a number of different observation recordings that demonstrated that Vicky did not give any toys or objects to other children at different times of the day or during different activities, we could then conclude that Vicky does not know how to share.

Analysing your observation recording is an essential part of the observation process. In this process it is important that all the Early Years team are involved, as well as parents or carers. 'The quality of the observations and of the analysis of these observations will determine the quality of assessment made' (Lally and Hurst 1992, p.79).

Lally and Hurst (1992) have developed a framework for analysing the recordings of the observations. They suggest a series of issues that will enable staff to start discussions around children's assessments.

- Acknowledge their previous experiences of the child and place observation in the context of this knowledge.

- Make use of their observations to inform their assessment record of the child.

- Raise further questions about the child's experiences. These may be in connection with the role of the provision, or of the involvement of other children or adults with the child. In this way one observation can be seen to inspire further investigation.

- Use the information to plan to support the child's future learning.

- Communicate with one another, as analysis of observations is shared (Lally and Hurst, 1992, p.90).

Obviously, working within the EYFS you operate under a framework for assessment. This can be translated into a series of questions to start your analysis of observation recordings:

- What does this observation recording tell us about each child's experiences and progress?

- What does this observation recording tells us about each child's interests, skills, development and learning achievements?

- What information do you still need to assess each child fully in order to complete the EYFS Profile?

- How will this observation recording help you to share information with the children, parents, other services in order to promote partnership?

- How will the observation recording help you to evaluate the implementation of your activities within EYFS?

- Has your observation recording met the aims and objectives of your observation design?

Prior to the completion of the assessment scales, there are steps to undertake in order to help you with the analysis of observation recordings. Firstly, having the development of the child as a guide, focus on an individual child and create a specific profile of his or her development. Within this framework you can make comparisons as to what extent the child has met certain developmental areas, what the strengths of the child are, and where you need to focus greater in order to enhance this child's development. For example, looking at a child's personal, emotional and social development, the EYFS' nine points can become your criteria of investigating where this child is developmentally.

Consequently, with a mixture of observation recording providing cumulative data, you can begin to build a profile of the child's progress throughout the EYFS. This way it assists you to plan appropriate activities and support this child's development and learning.

Secondly, you can refer back to the aims of observations that reflect the learning goals of EYFS, and try to compare your observation recordings alongside the aims of the learning goals. This will enable you to evaluate whether your activities have been implemented effectively based on a child's progress.

The final process is to consider the documentation of your findings. The next chapter offers a discussion on how observation recordings are filed, stored and documented.

C H A P T E R   S U M M A R Y

This chapter discussed the most common observation tools that the EYP can use to observe children, the education programme, and its activities. The observations are divided into participatory observation and non-participatory observation. The non-participatory observations include:

- written observation;
- checklists;
- diagrammatic observation;
- sampling.

Also emphasised was the importance of analysing the observation recordings in order to assist you in completing the statutory assessment scales of the EYFS.

The next chapter discusses the ethical implications of the observation process and explores how observation findings should be documented, by looking at different techniques and practices.

FURTHER READING

Riddall-Leech, S. (2005) *How to observe children*, Oxford: Heinemann Educational Publishers.

Salaman, A. and Tutchell, S. (2005) *Planning educational visits for the early years*, London: Sage.

Smidt, Sandra (2005) *Observing, assessing and planning for children in the early years*, London: Routledge.

4 Ethical implications

Introduction

This chapter aims to discuss the ethical implications of observing young children. It explains the role of the adult as a guardian to young children whilst data is being collected for assessment purposes. It emphasises the fact that before any observations are commenced, careful consideration must be given to young children's right to participate, and the ethics involved in observing young children for assessment and evaluation purposes. It will also discuss the importance of reporting data about a child to other professionals, and to parents, in an ethical manner. Documentation is essential in the process of reporting observations and a number of examples of these will be offered.

Ethics of the observation process

As it has been emphasised in previous chapters, observations should maintain a central role within Early Years practice. The role of observation processes to both children and to the educational programme should be the promotion of quality care and education that children receive, and also to enhance professional practice. Observations help the Early Years team to extend their understanding about their educational programme, in addition to their understanding of the children themselves. In order to consider the ethical implications involved in observations, it is essential to consider the purposes of observation in the Early Years.

The process of observing children in any Early Years environment should be characterised by the ethical considerations.

Early Years Professionals and practitioners, when they start the process of observation, should create an ethical framework around this process which is going to inform planning education programmes and assessments of each child. The ethical guidelines for the Early Years environment should underpin the work of Early Years Professionals. When we consider the ethics in the observation process there is a need to look at the involvement of the team, the parents and the children. It is also important to refer to:

- the reasons why we observe and keep records;
- how these records are kept; and
- subsequently how we share the information that we have collected.

The following paragraphs will attempt to discuss the ethical issues involved throughout the observation process.

Team involvement

Team involvement is the starting point during the observation process. As was explained in Chapter 3, the Early Years team meets and discusses the observation design, and the aims and objectives of the observation process itself. It is at this initial meeting that the creation of the ethical framework should occur. As part of the ethical procedure the members of the team need to agree to a code of practice amongst themselves which reflects the aims and the purposes for observation. Mutual respect, the creation of a work environment where all opinions are valued, and where everyone's expertise, interests and skills are encouraged and taken into consideration, are elements that create an ethical code between members of the team, where everyone feels safe, free and confident in getting involved and reflects the aims for observing young children within the EYFS framework.

The starting point is deciding what information will be collected. This is an important aspect for considering the ethical considerations of the observation design. Unnecessary collection of information with regard to children or to the educational programme should be avoided and/or limited. It is crucial for the observation process that the aims and objectives are well defined and explained. The aims and objectives of observations should not only be clarified, but also understood by all members of the Early Years team. The team needs to agree on the aims and objectives of the observation process. All the team members, in a meeting, should be able to express their views. The final result of the meeting is a decision with regard to the observation processes, techniques and methods, and the observation design should be a collaborative product. Within the observation design process the needs of the setting, as well as the needs of the children and the team members, should be met. These needs include:

- an agreement on the accessibility of the information;
- the filing and sharing of team members' observation recordings;
- an agreement upon who will share the information with the participants involved.

REFLECTIVE TASK

Consider in your setting whether there is a team meeting in place when observation processes are discussed and designed.

Parental involvement

One of the key procedures in establishing an ethical code is to gain parental involvement. The Early Years team has a challenging task, seeking not only parental consent but also parental involvement as well. Working in Early Years can be overwhelming as practitioners and professionals are busy implementing the curriculum, complying with legislation, and delivering the learning goals of the EYFS. It is important that despite the demands of the daily routine of the Early Years team that the involvement of parents in the observation process is prioritised. So parental involvement should not be limited to merely signing a consent form. Parents should be involved and participate when observations are designed as an integral part of the ethics of the observations.

The gathering of observational evidence is crucial for Early Years practice so that links can be made between the individual developmental needs and learning achievements and planning of appropriate activities and promote partnership working together. Parental involvement should be encouraged and parents should be invited in to allow in depth discussion with the practitioners. When parents are getting involved in the Early Years practice and activities from the beginning of the observation process, they can provide collaboration throughout the process. Parental participation and encouragement can become helpful co-operators in the observation process.

Parental involvement should be encouraged throughout the process of observation. Parents should have explained to them the aims and objectives of the process, and also be informed as to what the observation is about. The purpose of the observation process should be transparent and understandable to the parents. Emphasis should be placed on why observation is important in the daily practice of the Early Years, how it is going to benefit the education programme, and furthermore how it will inform the activities that benefit individuals and groups of children.

It is also central when seeking parental involvement to explain to the parents that they can have access to the observation records at all times throughout the process. Parental involvement ought to be a choice for the parents, and they should retain the right to withdraw their participation at any time.

A number of questions can help us to investigate the degree of parental involvement.

✓ Have the parents had the purposes of the observation process explained to them?

✓ Have the parents expressed their opinions, and been allowed to make any suggestions or alterations?

✓ Have the parents been reassured that they will be able to access the observation recordings as and when they wish?

✓ Have the parents had it explained to them that they will be involved regularly, and they will remain informed about the observation process?

REFLECTIVE TASK

Reflecting on your own setting, consider how parental involvement is obtained and what ethical procedures you have to involve parents in.

The following points highlight the steps Early Years Professionals should undertake to fulfil their responsibility for maintaining parental involvement.

✓ Parents are kept fully informed throughout the process.

✓ Parents are getting involved whilst the child's assessment profile is being created.

✓ Regular meetings with the parents are essential in the process of keeping those parents informed and in gaining their trust, commitment and participation.

There is a necessity for a constant flow of information from the Early Years team, and not only during parents' evenings or in parents' meetings. A small note or a photograph explaining what the child has done during a day can be a good starting point for a short discussion but, at the same time, it is a valid tool for continuous communication with the parents.

PRACTICAL TASK

Study the Welfare Requirements section of EYFS and try to reflect on how you can maintain parental involvement within your own setting.

Children's involvement

The UN Convention on the Rights of the Child (UN, 1989) set the standards for listening to children's voices and promoting children's involvement in any decision-making that involves them. Since the UN Convention there has been an emphasis on children having an increased control over the policies, services and curricula that concern them. As has already been explained, the ethics of observing children should apply to all participants in the observation process, and ought to apply throughout this process. Consequently, children need to be informed and have explained to them the purposes of the observation process.

The question for Early Years practitioners is at what age children are able to get involved in the process, and how can they be informed about the observation process effectively. When babies and young children are observed, especially before the age of two years, it is more difficult and challenging to involve them due to the children's limited understanding. Their involvement will be different. Practitioners are not going to expect the babies and toddlers to voice themselves. Practitioners can involve babies and toddlers by acknowledging their rights to be respected, treated with sensitivity and being responsive to behaviours that might indicate they do not wish to participate.

However, as children grow older and more aware (say, at around the age of three) the Early Years Professional and practitioner can seek to involve the children in the observation process. Play can become the best context for this and as a tool to seek consent and involvement from very young children. Role-play, and children's drawing and story time, can provide a helpful context for a child's involvement. For example, they can create a story about their feelings with regard to a certain activity, and they can illustrate this story with their own drawings. There are further advantages to child involvement, aside for its ethical value alone. When children have been made aware that observations take place it aids the professional in stepping back and becoming a systematic observer. When children are aware that this will happen they may be less likely to disturb the process. In addition, they know where to go when they need something. This way your role as an observer becomes easier and more effective. Moreover, children can participate, and from a very young age they can start taking control of the processes that involve them.

FRACTICAL TASK

1 *Think how you can involve toddlers (say at around the age of 26 months) when you try to observe how they use their growing vocabulary to interact with other children or adults.*

2 *Think how you can involve children (say at around the age of 40–60 months) when you try to observe why a child does not take turns and does not want to share.*

To summarise, ethical considerations should not be separate from the observation process but an integral part of it. Ethical considerations should underpin the whole of the observation process. Parental involvement, as well as child involvement, should not be limited to informed consent forms; parents and children should be invited into the process of observation and play an active role within it.

FRACTICAL TASK

The following list of questions can be used to check whether the ethics have been applied in the observation process that you have designed for observing children.

- *Has the whole team agreed with the aims and objectives of the observation process?*

- *Has the whole team agreed with the observation methods and techniques?*

- *Have the parents been informed and had the observation process fully explained to them?*

- *Have the children (where applicable) had the nature of the observations, including their aims, objectives, and what tools will be used, explained to them?*

- *Have you made clear that all members concerned in the observation process will have access to the material?*

- *Have you confirmed that all details will remain confidential?*

- *Do parents have the right to withdraw their permission at any time without explanation?*

- *Will parents have access to all the collected information?*

- *Has health and safety been considered?*

The role of the adult as a guardian

The Local Safeguarding Children Board Regulations (2006) were set up as part of the need to protect and promote children's welfare. The concept of 'safeguarding' children aims to protect children from bullying, discrimination and accidents, and ensuring access to all services. Additionally, the CAF intends to protect children in a variety of contexts when there is a concern, as well as when safeguarding issues that arise. So from a legislation perspective Early Years professionals have frameworks to work with, when there are cases where observation and assessment is necessary for the child's well-being.

Within the observation process in the Early Years setting the role of the adult as a guardian is to consider whether:

✓ the observations that take place are in the best interest of the child;

✓ the observations will help the education programme;

✓ the observations will help to understand the child's development;

✓ the observations will inform practice and promote children's learning;

✓ the safety and protection of children is ensured.

Managing the observation recordings

As has been discussed in earlier chapters, Early Years practitioners use observations to gain both an understanding of children's development and learning, and to inform the planning of the activities. Following the introduction of the EYFS with its pre-set learning outcomes and learning goals, the EYP must use formal and structured guidelines, working within a common framework of assessment scales. The EYFS details what information for each child will be gathered through observations in the assessment scales. It also explains the documentation process of observation recordings and offers clear guidelines of how children's profiles should be created. It states that records must be kept for 'the safe and efficient management of the settings and to meet the needs of the children' (DCSF, 2008a, p. 38). The data collected is regulated under the Data Protection Act of 1998 and the Freedom of Information Act of 2000. The EYFS offers guidance on how long records should be kept. It states that 'records relating to individual children should be retained for a reasonable period of time (for example, three years) after the children have left provision' (ibid., p. 40).

Moreover, with the introduction of CAF these guidelines are even more structured. The CAF does not aim to replace the everyday observations that take place in the Early Years setting, but does aim to protect children and prevent the harming of children.

The CAF has been developed around three steps. The first step is 'Preparation' to identify whether there might be a problem, and to decide whether to carry out a common assessment; the next step is to carry this assessment out, and the final step is to identify relevant support when working with other services.

PRACTICAL TASK

The Common Assessment Framework for Children and Young People: Practitioners' Guide provides a detailed framework when children are assessed (see p.15). Study these guidelines and try to list the ethical implications that are addressed in them.

Although there is a wealth of legislation and guidelines, the Early Years Professional has been left feeling that there is an increase in the workload. Brandon *et al.* (2006), in an evaluation of the implementation of the CAF, found that agencies responsible for the CAF did not find it easy to implement a holistic approach to assessment. Working with parents directly and safeguarding parental involvement was a major hurdle. Roles and responsibilities were not always distributed across all sectors, as well as not being clear. The conclusion was that the lack of clarity, clear guidance, and the range of skills required could lead to 'anxiety and frustration' among workers, and consequently could create conflict and a loss of professional confidence.

With that in mind, the Early Years Professional has been left confused in terms of how they can document and what the purpose of documentation of observation recordings is. Luff (2007) identifies this as a problem in the Early Years. She claims that observation recording and documentation should have a supportive role in children's learning and in the professional's practice. She argues that documentation should not be just the collection of a number of papers, or 'a paper exercise duty', but that it should add value to the educational programme and should be beneficial to the children's assessment.

An important part of the observation process, in addition to the ethical considerations, is the analysis of the observation recording and how these recordings are kept. How observation recording are kept/documented should be done in an ethical way. Documentation is part of these ethical concerns.

The remaining question to the Early Years Professional is how the observation recordings are documented. Where shall the Early Years Professional start? When observation recordings are collected to further our understanding of children's development and learning, as well as to inform practice, then the Early Years Professional should ask four main questions.

What is the purpose of record keeping?

The purpose of record keeping should be in line with the aims and objectives of the observation process itself. The purpose is to enable all participants, i.e. the Early Years team, parents and children, to monitor children's progress, and also to inform the educational programme.

Observation recordings help the Early Years team to ensure continuity in the Early Years practice, which is the ultimate goal of the observation process.

Assessing children's progress within the educational programme, and being able to reflect upon the education programme, will help the Early Years team to cover all of the developmental areas suggested by the EYFS, as well as maintaining an understanding of their practice.

What is the use of record keeping?

The observation process is an ongoing and continuous process. The continuous collection of information about a child or a group of children, and the educational programme, can provide evidence to support assessment and referrals, as requested by the CAF. All of this evidence can be used as a communication tool with the parents, as well as other professionals and authorities, such as Local Authorities (LAs) and Ofsted. Sharing evidence of practice is a helpful way of exploring new pedagogies and experiences that inform the education programme.

Who are the participants in the process of record keeping?

The ones that share an interest in the process are the Early Years team, the children and the parents, but also the authorities that the Early Years setting is accountable to.

Who has accessibility of record keeping?

Accessibility in the records should be determined by who has an interest in the process of record keeping, and it is also determined by the settings' particular legislation, as well as by national legislations. Parents, carers and outside agencies are the ones who will have an interest, as well as the Early Years team members.

Sharing observations

How these observations and records are shared with parents and/or carers is an important consideration, as accessibility in the observation recording is part of the ethical implications. Drummond (1993, p.10) says about the Early Years Professional's role and responsibilities that 'paramount among them is the responsibility to monitor the effects of their work so to as to ensure that their good intentions for children are raised'.

The Statutory Framework of the EYFS (DCSF, 2008a, pp. 38–40) provides clear guidelines of how each child's profiles can be created and how information can be shared. In this section we describe some examples of other practices. The aim is to consider these examples of documentation and sharing information, so that you can reflect on your own practice.

The Mosaic approach

The Mosaic project, as mentioned in Chapter 2, aimed to 'emphasise that listening [to children] is an active process, involving not just hearing but interpreting, constructing meaning and responding' (Clark and Moss, 2001, p.7). Children were involved in the process of planning their own learning by the practitioners listening to their voices and their own perspectives of their lives. The Mosaic approach aimed to enable them as 'co-constructors' towards the activities (Clark and Moss, 2001). In this study the discussion of documentation was determined by creating a dialogue among children, practitioners, older children, parents and researchers. The involvement of all participants was central. Dialogue about the documentation was shared in the following ways:

The idea of creating portfolios as tools of documentation was introduced. These portfolios were open ones and new tools or materials could be added with the participation of adults, parents and children. Whenever children's or adult's skills and interests were developing these were added to the portfolio. The important aspect of these portfolios were the data collection tools that were developed to enable children to express their views, ideas and feelings (Clark and Moss, 2001). Observation recordings were central in the Mosaic approach. Child conferencing – which took the form of a short interview – tours with the child, as well as the use of media techniques such as photographs and videos, were the basis for collecting information around children's interests and skills. Thus children's participation was central throughout the child conferencing technique.

In order to create these portfolios three important aspects were taken into consideration.

1 The tools that were used throughout the process of collecting information about children's perspectives of their own lives.

2 The view of the child as an 'expert' in his or her own life.

3 The involvement of all participants, and especially parents and key workers, was highly valued.

As a result, the Mosaic approach suggested a new way of documenting observation recordings for children. Working in an educational setting, assessment for children should not only focus on the developmental and educational goals, but should start from the child's perspectives, and should also emphasise the child's life experiences.

Reflect on your own practice, which is underpinned by EYFS, and consider whether you can adopt some of the ways the Mosaic approach used for documentation.

Will this be possible with the workload in your setting?

Will it promote children's and parents involvement and participation? If yes, in what ways?

Documentation in practice

Adapted from Luff. P. (2007): Written observation or walks in the park? Documenting children's experiences, in Moyles, J. (2007) Early years foundations: meeting the challenge, *Maidenhead: Open University Press.*

Effective documentation in practice

Documentation should enhance our walks in the park with children and not prevent them from happening. It is not necessary to record everything, to spend time producing masses of perfect paperwork which is filed away and rarely seen. It is important, however, to recognise that thinking and learning are not easily visible and that our memories are not unlimited. Writing down an observation, photocopying a drawing, or taking a photograph help us to bring learning into view, so that it can be seen, reflected upon and discussed. Three practical approaches to documentation are considered below. Any of these can be adapted, according to available resources, and used in a variety of Early Years settings.

Photo sequences

By taking a digital camera along to the park, staff may capture a sequence of photographs. These could be of a child gaining confidence on the climbing frame, or a small group of children finding and examining leaves and acorns. On returning to the nursery, even before these pictures are printed, children will love to sit with a practitioner and review the images on a computer screen (or, if available, via a data projector) recognising themselves, naming other children, remembering and taking about what they did on the walk. As soon as selected images are printed, they can be displayed in simple photograph albums or on the nursery walls, with or without captions. Children can then see and recall their actions; parents and visitors to the nursery have evidence of what happened during the walk in the park and may understand and comment on the learning that occurred, and the staff can use the pictures as a starting point of their discussions, evaluations and the planning of future outings.

Child profiles

A portfolio, or profile, compiled during a child's time during attending an Early Years setting can provide a very positive record of what that child can do and has achieved

(Driscoll and Rudge 2005). Kept in a scrapbook, document wallet or loose-leaf folder, such profiles might contain written observations, children's drawings and photographs of the child involved in activities. It is not possible or necessary to record everything in a profile but at key points during the child's time at nursery, as part of a process of regular occasional monitoring, on special occasions, or when something notable occurs, entries can be made. It is likely that a child's key worker will have the main responsibility for keeping the profile but will use it in an open and inclusive way, as an invaluable means of building relationships with the child and family and for creating and sustaining links between nursery and home. Children are proud of their profiles and can take decisions about what goes into them. They may want to include the leaf rubbing they did at the park, or the photograph of them pushing their friend on the swing. Parents are thrilled to see what their children are achieving at nursery and the profile can provide a stimulus to talk about what children are doing at home. The profile may be taken home and parents may add pictures or stories about family events. For parents, nursery staff and other professionals, the profile can be an invaluable document to review the child's strengths, understand their interests, and note the progress that has been made.

Learning stories

Practitioners, parents and children can also all be involved in contributing to learning stories. As with photo sequences and portfolios, this approach focuses upon positive outcomes emphasising each child's participation and their development of positive dispositions and attitudes towards learning. Observations are made, often recorded on prepared proformas. These provide space for an observation, or learning story, to be recorded and have sections for a short-term review, which allows the practitioner to offer an initial interpretation of the learning story. The observed story is then discussed and interpreted collaboratively and, along with photographs, work samples and comments from the child and parents, becomes the basis for decisions about the next steps for learning (Carr 2001). In this approach, the focus is upon the child as a learner within the Early Years setting with the recognition that their learning is supported and enhanced by the people and resources which pr mote the child's activity and thinking. If a notebook and camera are taken on the walk to the park, a simple learning story can be captured 'W. picked something up off the ground and said, "It's an acorn." He handed it to E. saying, "It's muddy. Can you get the mud off it?" When E. cleaned it and handed it back, he tried very hard to remove the shell from the acorn. He asked E. to break it open and then looked at the seed inside and said, "It's white."' Returning to the nursery, the short-term review may be that W. recognises the acorn and is curious to find out what's inside. Talking to other staff, to W. and his mother you may discover that W. is developing an interest in finding natural objects and you then might plan to collect and examine more acorns, to bring them back to nursery to look at more closely, with a magnifying glass, and perhaps plant some acorns to investigate their growth.

REFLECTIVE TASK

Reading the previous extract reflect on your own setting and discuss the following.

How much assessment is documented formally in your setting?

Who has access to this documentation, and how?

Is this type of documentation user-friendly for the parents and the children?

What methods do you use to document your observation recording?

CASE STUDY

Te Whaariki

Te Whaariki does not have a standardised approach to the documentation of observation recordings. Each setting decides to assess, and consequently document, observation recordings according to their own aims and objectives, and according to what purpose the assessment will be used for. Parents not only give their permission, but are also actively involved in the process.

Documentation in a Te Whaariki class involves: the observation findings, photographs, the transcripts of children's interactions either with their peers or with adults, and the children's own work. Ten reasons for documenting observation recording are described.

1 *To understand children's learning better, observations are looked at very carefully, and the process of writing these observations help the Early Years team to focus upon a child's development in order to understand that child's development better. It also aims to gain an insight into children's development and to understand the child's needs in order to help them.*

2 *To implement discussion of children's learning, as it is central to this curriculum that the starting point for discussing children's learning is their individual assessment.*

3 *It is a communication tool for sharing information with all the participants.*

4 *To assess how situations have been handled, adults and children's participation enables the Early Years practitioners to reflect on their practice.*

5 *In planning learning models for individuals and groups, an emphasis on the central role of assessment is to determine whether learning activities that have been designed do have an effect on children's learning and whether this learning is meeting their needs.*

6 *To ensure that all children receive attention, it is important to investigate whether all children have the necessary attention, and that no one child misses out on either being seen or heard. In the Early Years class some children tend to have more attention than others, thus the TE Whaariki documentation of observation recordings*

attempts to ensure that all children share the same amount of consideration. Important tools for this are the 'learning stories', which enable Early Years practitioners to plan the development of positive interests and skills.

7   *To highlight the learning that is valued in the setting, Early Years practitioners develop activities within the Te Whaariki curriculum. Documentation of observations recording enables practitioners to gain an insight into children's understanding of these values, and it is a way of directly involving children in the process, as children subsequently acquire an understanding of the meanings and purposes of the activities.*

8   *To involve children in self-assessment, encouraging children to assess themselves. helps the Early Years Professional to enable children to take ownership of their own learning, and for them to make choices of what work goes into their portfolios or files, therefore evaluating their own efforts. However, it is acknowledged that self evaluation of children can have its pitfalls, as it can lead to lack of response in terms of spontaneity from children, and can increase an attitude towards performance-driven behaviours in children, rather than exploration (which is a central premise to Te Whaariki).*

9   *To involve the parents in a discussion of assessment information. When families are informed their input and involvement increase, and this can subsequently help to meet the outcomes of the education programme.*

10   *To share experiences with the family, the 'Learning Stories', as a tool for sharing information, cannot only make very interesting reading to the families of their children's experience within the setting, but also to share what their children are doing within the early childhood setting (Carr, 1998, 1999, 2001).*

Reflecting on how EYFS Assessment Scales are used, can you identify any of these purposes for observation of the practice in your setting?

CHAPTER SUMMARY

This chapter raises some issues on ethical implications when young children are observed. Within the new policy initiatives, reforms, legislation and curriculum, the Early Years sector has a number of reference points with regard to ethical practices.

However, it is argued in this chapter that ethical implications are not about consent, but are about involvement from all participants in the observation process. Observation processes should be underpinned by careful consideration of the ethical issues, and documentation is important to these ethical discussions. The three examples of practices, the Mosaic approach, documenting children's experiences, and Te Whaariki, all demonstrate how the observation process can be documented in a way which enables the participation of children and parents. They are also examples of how documentation can be used to share information with whoever has an interest in children's development and learning, in an informal way which benefits children, workers and parents.

Carr M. (1998) *Assessing children's learning in early childhood settings: a development programme for discussion and reflection*, Wellington: New Zealand Council for Educational Research.

Carr, M., (2001) *Assessment in early childhood settings*, London: Paul Chapman Publishing.

Clark, A. and Moss, P. (2001) *Listening to young children: the Mosaic approach*, London: National Children's Bureau.

Luff, P. (2007) Written observations or walks in the park: documenting children's experiences, in J. Moyles, (ed.) *Early years foundations: meeting the challenge*, Maidenhead: Open University Press.

5 Observing for development

CHAPTER OBJECTIVES

By the end of this chapter you should be able to:
- consider how we observe children's development;
- consider how we observe children's learning and play;
- link observations to the Assessment Scales of the EYFS.

This chapter addresses the following Standards for EYPS: S1, S10 and S12.

Introduction

In the previous chapters the role of observation and the observational methods, as well as the ethical implications that are an integral part of them, were explored. As has been discussed previously, observations should become part of the everyday life in the Early Years setting, being 'woven' into the setting's activities and with children's interactions with other children and with adults. This chapter discusses the role of observations in children's development and learning, with an emphasis on play, and links observations to the EYFS learning goals.

What do we know about children's development?

In Chapter 1 an overview of theories about children's development was offered, drawing the conclusion that our Early Years practice is influenced by these theories and by how children are viewed in the social and cultural context. Child development is rooted in moral, social and political choices and problems (Hartley, 1993). These ideas about early childhood result in different approaches to the subject of child development. Understanding why and how children develop in the Early Years is crucial to professionals, as it influences their approaches to children. Child development is about 'anticipation, attainment and assessment' (Robinson, 2008, p.3). The developmental achievements of children are central to Early Years practice and are important for children's progression in life, as through development children acquire skills and abilities which they will use for the rest of their lives. Consequently, the ways observations are designed are shaped by how we think about children's development.

The Early Years Foundation Stage maintains a 'holistic' view of child development, and describes the different aspects of this development according to four main themes: the healthy child, the competent learner, the skilful communicator and the 'strong' child. While there is an emphasis on the holistic approach to children, traditionally development is studied in these separate areas.

- physical and biological development;
- social and emotional development;
- cognitive development;
- language development.

This helps professionals to understand, in a deeper and more effective way, how children develop. However, even though we study development in these separate areas, these often interlink and impact upon each other.

There is a wealth of literature and research on child development that the Early Years Professional can use to seek guidance and advice. Central to all developmental theories that seek to expand knowledge and understanding of how children develop are observations. *I*Observation recordings and information are valuable resources when examining child development.*I*Observation techniques are key to the study of child development. The information collected by different observation techniques provides insights into many aspects of child development.

However, because of the limitations of each technique for gathering information, many techniques are used in combination to study children and to understand their behaviour. For example, when you look at a child's emotional development you might want to combine observation techniques such as a checklist, time sampling and narratives. Even in this case the information that you collect might not be complete. As a result it is very important to discuss your findings and concerns with parents, in order to gain a better understanding of where a certain type of behaviour occurs. You can then make conclusions about a child's progress in a certain developmental area.

CASE STUDY

Ben is 2 years and 16 days old. He has just moved to a village with his mother, father and his older sister. His sister attends the same nursery as him. Ben's mother provided the nursery with his portfolio from his previous nursery, which Ben attended from nine months old. The checklists in his portfolio highlighted Ben's development, with a particular focus on his physical development and his language development. The nursery staff have already identified that Ben enjoys building, which he will do in the construction area, or the sand or water areas, and whenever he gets the opportunity to build things up high he will. However, the staff have noticed that he prefers to do this on his own, and that he stops doing this when other children join him.

After a team meeting the staff in the nursery decided to observe Ben to collect further information about him, in order to identify at what stage he is at developmentally, and also to focus on his social skills, in order to encourage him to interact more with other children.

They decided to observe him every day for a week. The main focus of the observation was social development and the objectives were to observe Ben's interactions with other children during play and activities. They decided to carry out time and event samplings, tracking and narratives. The narratives take place in two formats: as participant observations if something occurs, and also as non-participant observations. The staff in Ben's group share roles, in order to know when they will observe him. They felt that in this way they could collect the information they need to effectively assess his social skills.

Before starting systematic observations of Ben the staff undertook some further reading on social and emotional development.

Some notes on what we know about social and emotional development:

The Early Years in a child's life are important for the formation of personal, social and emotional development. An environment that is safe, affectionate and encouraging promotes positive feelings in children and develops their social skills. From the moment children are born they are engaged in interacting with adults in an attempt to become independent and social beings. The early stages of their lives are important for the acquisition of the social and emotional skills that will enhance their personal development.

We tend to study social and emotional development together as they are interlinked and reinforce each other. Social development has two important aspects. Firstly, children attempt to form an identity and a personality through differentiating themselves as distinctive individuals and, secondly, they try to find a place in the immediate social community and in society at large. From the beginning of life children try to develop their 'self concept', or an image of themselves: 'It is a cognitive construction [. . .] a system of describing and evaluating representations about the self' (Harter, 1996, p.207). The attainment of the concept of self involves the development of a self-image, which is an attempt to understand ourselves and to gain an inner picture of who we are. This acquisition of self-esteem is a process whereby we come to an understanding of our self-worth and value. In the complex process of developing a concept of the self we are required to achieve appropriate socialisation skills that enable us to interact with our environment. Understanding shared values, beliefs and rules, we make attempts to get to know our social environment and to try to fit into our community.

Emotional development is concerned with our feelings, and how we control these feelings in order to respond appropriately on different occasions. Emotions are internal or external reactions to certain situations, and will differ from child to child. For example, when a child gets angry they might express their anger by crying, whereas another child might express anger by becoming sad and withdrawn.

One of the most influential theories about children's emotional development, and one which is very relevant to the Early Years, is attachment theory, initially developed by Bowlby. Attachment is the bond between the mother or carer and the baby. Secure relationships with the family help children to form positive relationships with others. It is important to understand attachment theory, as children who come to the Early Years setting from a very young age are asked to separate from their parents or carers and spend time in the Early Years setting instead. Some children experience this separation as a distressing situation and become upset.

It is also important to understand that children's emotional responses have not yet matured and, subsequently, they are not able to maintain control over their feelings of distress, anger, sadness, interest, affection or joy. Thus the Early Years environment is important in helping children to be able to express their emotions and, at the same time, to also provide opportunities for assisting children to move towards controlling their feelings and expressing them through words.

Table 5.1 Examples from Ben's event sampling observation

Time	Activity	Social Group	Comments
12:00–12:02	Ben sits at the table with two other boys and two girls. The nursery nurse is pouring them all a drink. The children are encouraged to say 'thank you'. Ben says this but sits quietly at the table as the other children talk.	2 boys 2 girls	When Ben is encouraged to speak he does. However, he does not feel confident enough to speak to the other children.
12:30–12:32	Ben is washing his hands because they are covered in yogurt. He returns to the table and sits quietly next to a girl.	2 boys 1 girl	Ben shows that he is capable of washing his own hands without help from the staff, but he does not interact with the other children in the bathroom or at the table.

CASE STUDY *continued*

1:00–1:02	The children are singing nursery rhymes and songs. They are sitting on the carpet during the last few minutes of the session. Ben is joining in with singing and arm actions. The nursery nurse has asked the children to pair up so they can sing 'row, row, row your boat' and rock backwards and forwards holding each other's hands. Ben remains sitting still on the carpet. The nursery nurse moves Jack over to Ben and partners them up. The two boys hold hands. The singing begins. Ben is not singing but is carrying out the actions. The children are laughing when the nursery rhymes have finished. They sing the nursery rhyme again, to which Ben joins in and is smiling and laughing at the end.	All children 1 nursery nurse	Ben seems to enjoy the activity. However, he also seems to become uncomfortable when partnered up. When given another opportunity to participate in the nursery rhyme Ben has relaxed more and joins in with the other children.
1:30–1:32	There are different play-stations set up around the room and staff are helping children to make a winter picture on the arts table. Ben is playing in the sandpit on his own. He is building a sandcastle.	Solitary play	Ben is choosing to play alone. Other children are playing alongside each other and together on the carpet with cars and trains, but Ben does not join them.
2:00–2:02	Ben is on the carpet in the corner with a box of 'Duplo' bricks and he is building with the yellow pieces. Jack has come over and has also started taking Duplo bricks out of the box. Ben stops playing. After 30 seconds Jack hands Ben a yellow piece that he has pulled out of the box. 'Oh look, yellow', he says. 'Thanks,' Ben replies, taking the piece. He looks at Jack and he picks up two more pieces.	Solitary play, and then parallel play with Jack	Ben still seems wary of what other children are doing, but perhaps this is because it is only his second week in this group. It is positive to see that Ben is able to play alongside Jack with the same toys.
2:30–2:32	The nursery nurse calls Ben and Jack over to make their Christmas pictures. Ben is talking to the nursery nurses quite confidently and, when asked which colours he wants in his picture, he keeps saying the same colours as Jack wants to use.	Jack Nursery nurse	Ben appears to listen to what Jack says and he repeats the same colours. It might be an attempt to 'share' with Jack.

93

3:00–3:02	Ben is playing in the sand area on his own again. Jack is also present. A girl has begun to play at the opposite side of the sand tray. Jack continues to play with his bucket and spade. 'Where have all spades gone?' she asks. Jack bends underneath the tray and passes a spade to the girl.	Sand area Ben and Jack	Ben plays alongside with Jack, yet he does not seem to be interacting with Jack or sharing with him, but he stays there even when another child arrives to play.
3:30–3:32	The children are sitting all together on the carpet listening to the nursery nurse reading from a 'Big Book'. Ben is sitting next to Jack and he pays attention to the story being read.	All children in the room with the nursery nurse	Although Ben is listening to the story, he has chosen to sit next to Jack.
4:00–4:02	Ben is asleep on large beanbags.		Ben is usually picked up at 3:30 but his mother said she would be late, so the nursery staff have let him sleep.
4:30–4:32	Ben is woken up by his mother and he smiles when he sees her. His mother puts his jacket on, collects his bag and carries him out of the room. Ben turns his head and says, 'Bye, Jack.' He raises his left hand to wave 'goodbye' to Jack.	Mother Nursery nurse Jack is present	Ben has shown a positive sign by waving to Jack. It seems that he is starting to like Jack and is showing an interest in socialising with him.

Table 5.2 Event sampling (example taken from half a day that Ben was in the nursery)

Behaviours	Carpet area	Construction area	Water tray	Role play area	Sand tray
Ben talks to another child	* *	* ***	**	******	*
Ben does not talk to another child	*********	***********	**********	***************	*************
Ben plays alongside another child	************	*****************	*************	************	*******************
Ben leaves when another child arrives	**	**********	**********	******	****

Collecting a number of observation recordings (above are only two of a variety of examples that were carried out within the space of a week), staff analysed the information. They concluded that Ben is making progress in terms of interacting with others and that he has started settling into the new setting and is making positive progress in towards his social development. It appears from the observation recordings that it may take a while longer before he becomes completely relaxed and confident with his new situation, but he will eventually become more familiar with the new routine. The staff looked at developmental stages and they concluded that Ben plays in parallel to other children, and that he has not yet moved to play co-operatively. The staff decided to discuss all the observation findings with his parents and to ask them their opinion.

What do we know about children's learning?

The Early Years learning environment is dominated by a play-orientated pedagogy. A number of studies (Moyles, et al., 2001, Sylva et al., 2001, Siraj-Blatchford and Sylva, 2002, Taylor et al., 2002) found that children's learning is enhanced in settings where there is a balance between both adult and child-initiated activities. Learning is also enhanced where practice is planned within a framework of observation and assessment, with parental involvement, and by liaising with other services.

In Chapter 1 it was discussed that in order to create a learning environment for children some conditions of learning need to be taken into consideration. These are as follows.

- Emphasis on children's development.

- Emphasis on play.

- Emphasis on children's needs.

- Emphasis on children's freedom to choose materials and activities.

- Emphasis on children's ownership of their own learning.

However, these conditions are not directly linked to children's learning alone. The role of the adult is also important, as learning will not occur in an environment where these conditions exist without the support of adults. Children's early experiences can be enhanced by the interaction of adults during their play.

Play underpins the EYFS. It is suggested that adults hold a key role in assisting children's play both indoors and outdoors. It is recognised that children 'play spontaneously, although some may need adult support, and it is through play that they develop intellectually, creatively, physically and emotionally'. (DCSF, 2008b, p. 7)

Through play children acquire skills within a given context. A number of studies on play and learning (Athey, 1990, 2007, Nutbrown, 1999) suggest that children are able to develop planned and purposeful play, and the role of the adult is to base the planning for the educational programme on this. These studies point out that learning through play can be put at risk in a framework where learning outcomes are target driven. As mentioned in Chapter 1, play for a young child is spontaneous and lacks organisation. Consequently learning through play can become unpredictable, as children's interests or needs may take unplanned and unforeseen directions. These, however, are valid learning opportunities for children, as they build upon their own interests and needs, and the children take ownership of their own play and learning. The role of the adult is crucial in such an environment that values play as enabling children to be creative and playful in their ideas. Professionals' support, intervention, interaction and planning can assist children's play and can enable children to benefit developmentally from that play.

In a play-based learning environment observations are equally important and integral to constantly monitoring children's progress. Observations can become a valuable tool to collect information in context, and to ensure that the assessment of children will be meaningful. Such assessments will demonstrate not only what children can do and what different skills children have acquired, but also how they use those skills.

Working within a framework such as the Early Years Foundation Stage has some constraints, as intended learning outcomes are not always realistically observable and measurable, nor are they easily achieved by children. Observing children's learning for assessment purposes in an environment with set learning goals requires:

- communication with parents, in order to set appropriate expectations from both sides, and to involve parents in the observation process;

- space and resources applicable to the adult/child ratio;

- time built in for effective team meetings and the preparation of the observations' design;

- the development of effective observation systems and record keeping;

- training.

CASE STUDY

Louise is two years and eight months. She attends nursery three times per week. In the following observation the tracking technique has been used. It not only demonstrates Louise's preferences during play, but also how she uses her social skills during it.

Start 2:10 (15 minutes in carpet area)

Sitting on the carpet with a friend. Louise is showing her friend photographs and narrates what she was doing when these photographs were taken (from her summer holidays).

2:25 (8 minutes, water tray area)

Louise and her friend move to the water area and they are sorting out different shells into groups. Louise's friend leaves her and goes to the sand tray. After two minutes Louise also leaves but she does not follow her friend.

CASE STUDY *continued*

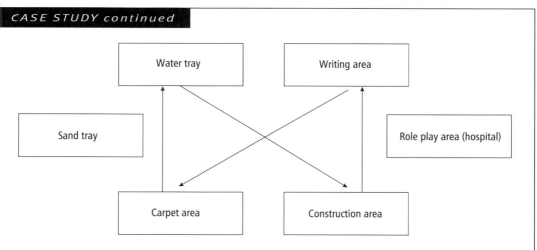

Figure 5.1 Louise's preference of play areas

2:33 *(13 minutes in the construction area)*

Louise plays on her own and she creates a strong well-built model using magnetic blocks.

2:46 *(14 minutes in the writing area)*

Louise sits at a table with two other children. She has chosen to colour in a picture of a 'Gruffalo'. She is doing this with care, and at the same time she talks to other children.

Finish 3:00 Children are called to the carpet area and Louise goes there with her picture.

Linking observations to the Early Years Foundation Stage

As mentioned in Chapter 1, the EYFS aims to:

- meet the diverse needs of the child;
- promote partnership working;
- provide flexible provision;
- create activities for children through play;
- improve the quality of provision for children.

Among the statutory duties, the Early Years Foundation Stage places emphasis on:

- observation of children, in order to identify their needs, interests and their skills and abilities;
- recording children's responses in different situations;

- analysing observation recordings in order to identify children's achievements, or to identify areas where children need further support;

- involving the parents as part of the ongoing observation assessment process (EYFS, 2008).

The Early Years Foundation Stage defines assessments of children as being an analysis of what you know about an individual child in terms of that child's development and learning. The purpose of the assessment in the EYFS is to:

- make informed decisions about the child's progress;

- plan your activities to meet the needs of children.

The EYFS suggests two types of assessment

The first, 'Formative assessments' are based on observations, and use techniques such as photographs, video recordings, children's drawings and information from parents. Observation recordings form a picture of the everyday life of children in the Early Years setting. They provide rich information for formative evidence, to base future planning on and to extend your knowledge and understanding of how children develop and learn, as well as providing evidence of their developing competencies, persistent interests, dispositions and schemas (Katz and Chard, 1989, Athey, 1990, 2007). Therefore it is important for observations to be an integral part of Early Years practice and activity. Observations are not the final process in a curriculum, but part of the actions of Early Years Professionals and practitioners for constantly improving quality within the setting. Formative assessments based on observation recordings assist the EYP to:

- offer a flexible provision for children, where activities are changed when children lack interest in them, and plans are altered to follow children's interests and needs, and where new activities take place to rekindle children's interests;

- provide evidence for starting communications with the parents, and to encourage parental involvement;

- provide evidence for communicating with other services and local authorities.

For effective formative assessment it is important to make observations:

- integral and a regular part of life in the setting;

- incidental, when something is happening outside of planned activities;

- during activities with children.

The second type of assessment is 'summative assessment'. In the EYFS it is a statutory requirement that each child will have a summative assessment at the end of the EYFS. This is a final assessment, which includes a summary of all the formative assessments undertaken over a long period of time, and offers a more holistic picture of a child's development and learning. It is stated in the EYFS (DCSF, 2008a) that each profile will include information about the child's progress towards the stated early learning goals.

The summative assessment is equally as important as the formative assessment. It is not only used to communicate with local authorities and for inspection purposes: it is also a very helpful tool as it assists:

- transitions from one Early Years setting to another, and transitions to Key Stage 1;

- professionals and practitioners to evaluate the activities and their implementation;

- approaches to other agencies with informed evidence, if required.

As can be seen in both types of assessments, observations are vital to professionals and practitioners in all areas of Early Years practice. Observation skills need to be developed from a very early stage in practitioner's training.

The formative and summative assessments of children are a statutory part of the Assessment and Reporting Arrangements within the EYFS. The EYFS suggests 13 Assessment scales, each of which has nine points that are linked to developmental areas. These are:

Assessment scales

Assessment scales (Statutory Framework for the Early Years Foundation Stage, 2008, pp.44–48)

Personal, social and emotional development

Dispositions and attitudes

1 Shows an interest in classroom activities through observation or participation.

2 Dresses, undresses and manages own personal hygiene with adult support.

3 Displays high levels of involvement in chosen activities.

4 Dresses and undresses independently and manages own personal hygiene.

5 Selects and uses activities and resources independently.

6 Continues to be interested, motivated and excited to learn.

7 Is confident to try new activities, initiate ideas and speak in a familiar group.

8 Maintains attention and concentration.

9 Sustains involvement and perseveres, particularly when trying to solve a problem or reach a satisfactory conclusion.

Social development

1 Plays alongside others.

2 Builds relationships through gestures and talking.

3 Takes turns and shares with adult support.

4 Works as part of a group or class, taking turns and sharing fairly.

5 Forms good relationships with adults and peers.

6 Understands that there needs to be agreed values and codes of behaviour for groups of people, including adults and children, in order to work together harmoniously.

7 *Understands that people have different needs, views, cultures and beliefs, which need to be treated with respect.*

8 *Understands that s/he can expect others to treat her or his needs, view, culture and beliefs with respect.*

9 *Takes account of the ideas of others.*

Emotional development

1 *Separates from main carer with support.*

2 *Communicates freely about home and community.*

3 *Expresses needs and feelings in appropriate ways.*

4 *Responds to significant experiences, showing a range of feelings when appropriate.*

5 *Has a developing awareness of own needs, views and feelings, and is sensitive to the needs, views and feelings of others.*

6 *Has a developing respect for own culture and beliefs and those of other people.*

7 *Considers the consequences of words and actions for self and others.*

8 *Understands what is right, what is wrong, and why.*

9 *Displays a strong and positive sense of self-identity, and is able to express a range of emotions fluently and appropriately.*

Communication, language and literacy

Language for communication and thinking

1 *Listens and responds.*

2 *Initiates communication with others, displaying greater confidence in more informal contexts.*

3 *Talks activities through, reflecting on and modifying actions.*

4 *Listens with enjoyment to stories, songs, rhymes and poems, sustains attentive listening and responds with relevant comments, questions or actions.*

5 *Uses language to imagine and recreate roles and experiences.*

6 *Interacts with others in a variety of contexts, negotiating plans and activities and taking turns in conversation.*

7 *Uses talk to organise, sequence and clarify thinking, ideas, feelings and events, exploring the meanings and sounds of new words.*

8 *Speaks clearly and with confidence and control, showing awareness of the listener.*

9 *Talks and listens confidently and with control, consistently showing awareness of the listener by including relevant detail. Uses language to work out and clarify ideas, showing control of a range of appropriate vocabulary.*

Linking sounds and letters

1 *Joins in with rhyming and rhythmic activities.*

2 *Shows an awareness of rhyme and alliteration.*

3 *Links some sounds to letters.*

4 *Links sounds to letters, naming and sounding letters of the alphabet.*

5 *Hears and says sounds in words.*

6 *Blends sounds in words.*

7 *Uses phonic knowledge to read simple regular words.*

8 *Attempts to read more complex words, using phonic knowledge.*

9 *Uses knowledge of letters, sounds and words when reading and writing independently.*

Reading

1 *Is developing an interest in books.*

2 *Knows that print conveys meaning.*

3 *Recognises a few familiar words.*

4 *Knows that, in English, print reads from left to right and top to bottom.*

5 *Shows an understanding of the elements of stories, such as main character, sequence of events and openings.*

6 *Reads a range of familiar and common words and simple sentences independently.*

7 *Retells narratives in the correct sequence, drawing on language patterns of stories.*

8 *Shows an understanding of how information can be found in non-fiction texts to answer questions about where, who, why and how.*

9 *Reads books of own choice with some fluency and accuracy.*

Writing

1 *Experiments with mark-making, sometimes ascribing meaning to the marks.*

2 *Uses some clearly identifiable letters to communicate meaning.*

3 *Represents some sounds correctly in writing.*

4 *Writes own name and other words from memory.*

5 *Holds a pencil and uses it effectively to form recognisable letters, most of which are correctly formed.*

6 *Attempts writing for a variety of purposes, using features of different forms.*

7 *Uses phonic knowledge to write simple regular words and make phonetically plausible attempts at more complex words.*

8 *Begins to form captions and simple sentences, sometimes using punctuation.*

9 *Communicates meaning through phrases and simple sentences with some consistency in punctuating sentences.*

Problem solving, reasoning and numeracy

Numbers as labels and for counting

1 *Says some number names in familiar contexts, such as nursery rhymes.*

2 *Counts reliably up to three everyday objects.*

3 *Counts reliably up to six everyday objects.*

4 *Says numbers in order.*

5 *Recognises numerals 1 to 10.*

6 *Counts reliably up to 10 everyday objects.*

7 *Orders numbers, up to 10.*

8 *Uses developing mathematical ideas and methods to solve practical problems.*

9 *Recognises, counts, orders, writes and uses numbers up to 20.*

Calculating

1 *Responds to vocabulary involved in addition and subtraction in rhymes and games.*

2 *Recognises differences in quantity when comparing sets of objects.*

3 *Finds one more or one less from a group of up to five objects.*

4 *Relates addition to combining two groups.*

5 *Relates subtraction to taking away.*

6 *In practical activities and discussion, begins to use the vocabulary involved in adding and subtracting.*

7 *Finds one more or one less than a number from 1 to 10.*

8 *Uses developing mathematical ideas and methods to solve practical problems.*

9 *Uses a range of strategies for addition and subtraction, including some mental recall of number bonds.*

Shape, space and measure

1 *Experiments with a range of objects and materials, showing some mathematical awareness.*

2 *Sorts or matches objects and talks about sorting.*

3 *Describes shapes in simple models, pictures and patterns.*

4 *Talks about, recognises and recreates simple patterns.*

5   *Uses everyday words to describe position.*

6   *Uses language such as 'circle' or 'bigger' to describe the shape and size of solids and flat shapes.*

7   *Uses language such as 'greater', 'smaller', 'heavier' or 'lighter' to compare quantities.*

8   *Uses developing mathematical ideas and methods to solve practical problems.*

9   *Uses mathematical language to describe solid (3D) objects and flat (2D) shapes.*

Knowledge and understanding of the world

1   *Shows curiosity and interest by exploring surroundings.*

2   *Observes, selects and manipulates objects and materials. Identifies simple features and significant personal events.*

3   *Identifies obvious similarities and differences when exploring and observing. Constructs in a purposeful way, using simple tools and techniques.*

4   *Investigates places, objects, materials and living things by using all the senses as appropriate. Identifies some features and talks about those features s/he likes and dislikes.*

5   *Asks questions about why things happen and how things work. Looks closely at similarities, differences, patterns and change.*

6   *Finds out about past and present events in own life, and in those of family members and other people s/he knows. Begins to know about own culture and beliefs and those of other people.*

7   *Finds out about and identifies the uses of everyday technology and uses information and communication technology and programmable toys to support his/ her learning.*

8   *Builds and constructs with a wide range of objects, selecting appropriate resources, tools and techniques and adapting her/his work where necessary.*

9   *Communicates simple planning for investigations and constructions and makes simple records and evaluations of her/his work. Identifies and names key features and properties, sometimes linking different experiences, observations and events. Begins to explore what it means to belong to a variety of groups and communities.*

Physical development

1   *Moves spontaneously, showing some control and coordination.*

2   *Moves with confidence in a variety of ways, showing some awareness of space.*

3   *Usually shows appropriate control in large and small-scale movements.*

4   *Moves with confidence, imagination and safety. Travels around, under, over and through balancing and climbing equipment. Shows awareness of space, of self and others.*

5 *Demonstrates fine motor control and coordination.*

6 *Uses small and large equipment, showing a range of basic skills.*

7 *Handles tools, objects, construction and malleable materials safely and with basic control.*

8 *Recognises the importance of keeping healthy and the things that contribute to this. Recognises the changes that happen to her/his body when s/he is active.*

9 *Repeats, links and adapts simple movements, sometimes commenting on her/his work. Demonstrates coordination and control in large and small movements, and in using a range of tools and equipment.*

Creative development

1 *Explores different media and responds to a variety of sensory experiences. Engages in representational play.*

2 *Creates simple representations of events, people and objects and engages in music making.*

3 *Tries to capture experiences, using a variety of different media.*

4 *Sings simple songs from memory.*

5 *Explores colour, texture, shape, form and space in two or three dimensions.*

6 *Recognises and explores how sounds can be changed. Recognises repeated sounds and sound patterns and matches movements to music.*

7 *Uses imagination for art and design, music, dance, imaginative role-play and stories. Responds in a variety of ways to what s/he sees, hears, smells, touches and feels.*

8 *Expresses and communicates ideas, thoughts and feelings using a range of materials, suitable tools, imaginative role-play, movement, designing and making, and a variety of songs and musical instruments.*

9 *Expresses feelings and preferences in response to artwork, drama and music, and makes some comparisons and links between different pieces. Responds to own work and that of others when exploring and communicating ideas, feelings and preferences through art, music, dance, role-play and imaginative play.*

Linking observations with the Early Years Professional

Working with children in the Early Years requires a number of skills, such as a good understanding and theoretical knowledge of child development, a good understanding of children's abilities and how they learn from play, as well as an understanding of effective pedagogy, and administrative skills. Among these skills the EYP needs very good observation skills, as the observation recordings offer insights into children's development and learning, and also enables the professional to create appropriate learning environments whilst working within the curriculum.

It is vital for the EYP to understand the theoretical underpinnings of one's own practice. The view of the child as a confident learner, able to choose his or her materials and activities, will determine the observation process. You then need to look at the child's development and what they are able to do at a given stage of their lives. This knowledge may result from literature on general aspects of development, but also from direct observations of children themselves. Knowing the individual children in your group, and their abilities, interests and needs, is the starting point for planning new activities and experiences. The main tools of validation are observations of children, taking into account both parental and child involvement. The observation recording will then be interpreted and become important information for assessing Early Years practice. These findings are an important tool to share with parents and children, in order to encourage and enable the children's participation in classroom life.

C H A P T E R   S U M M A R Y

This chapter discussed observations in relation to children's development and learning. Observations offer us information and evidence for understanding and extending our knowledge of children's development and learning. Observing for development and learning through play has some constraints, as it requires time and a high level of skills from the professional. However, they are valid tools as they assist every day practice with children.

Working within the Early Years Foundation Stage there is a clear emphasis on observation and assessment for children, for formative and summing-up purposes. Within this framework the EYP has to demonstrate skills and effective practice in observing young children, and also to lead and support the development of observation skills in others. The role of the EYP is challenging in the context of new policies and the implementation of the EYFS. The next chapter will discuss the role of the EYP in relation to observations.

FURTHER READING

Beaty, J. (2005) *Observing for development in young children*, New York: Macmillan.

Hobart, C. and Frankel, J. (2004) *A practical guide to child observations and assessments* (3rd edn), Cheltenham: Stanley Thornes.

Pratt, David (1994) *Curriculum planning: a handbook for professionals* (2nd edn), Fort Worth: Harcourt Brace.

6 The role of the Early Years Professional and observation

CHAPTER OBJECTIVES

By the end of this chapter you should be able to:
- reflect on your role within the Early Years learning environment;
- reflect on your role with regards to current policy and legislation;
- reflect on your role as the person responsible for the implementation of the Early Years Foundation Stage.

This chapter addresses the following Standards for EYPS: S1, S5, S6, S30, S33 and S36.

Introduction

This chapter summarises the main role of observation in Early Years practice in relation to the role of the Early Years Professional. It looks at the role of the EYP in the context of policy, and of the role of the EYP as an educator. It highlights the importance of observations as a means for implementing policies, as well as a means for understanding children, and in creating appropriate learning environments.

The context of the Early Years Professional

In the introductory chapter it became clear that services for children and families have been changing, as have quality standards for the Early Years sector. The introduction of the Early Years Professional Status was part of a wider government plan for children's services. The Common Core of Skills and Knowledge sets out basic standards that practitioners in the children's workforce need in order to work effectively with children and families (HM Government, 2006a). These skills help all practitioners to meet the 'working together' philosophy of Government policy. The skills and knowledge required are described under six headings.

- effective communication and engagement with children, young people and families;

- children's and young peoples' development;

- safeguarding and promoting the welfare of the child;

- supporting transitions;

- multi agency working;

- sharing information.

The Government announced that they expected all people working in the field of children's services, and supporting families, to have a basic level of competence in these six areas of the Common Core (HM Government, 2006a). Under the 'child and young people development' section one of the main skills that the new children's workforce should demonstrate is observation and judgements. This involves being able to do the following.

- *Observe a child or young person's behaviour, understand its context, and notice any unexpected changes.*

- *Listen actively, and respond to, concerns expressed about developmental or behavioural changes.*

- *Record observations in an appropriate manner.*

- *Understand that babies, children and young people see and experience the world in different ways.*

- *Evaluate the situation, taking into consideration the individual, their cicumstances and their development issues.*

- *Be able to recognise the signs of a possible developmental delay.*

- *Be able to support children and young people with a developmental difficulty or disability, and understand that their families, parents and carers will also need support and reassurance.*

- *Make considered decisions about whether concerns can be addressed by providing or signposting additional sources of information or advice.*

- *Where you feel that further support is needed, know when to take action yourself and when best to refer to managers, supervisors and other relevant professionals.*

- *Be able to distinguish between fact and opinion.*

The development of the postgraduate (Level 7) qualification – the National Professional Qualification for Integrated Children's Centre Leadership (NPQICL) – for practitioners who lead the multi-professional Children's Centres. The National Standards for Children's Centre leaders 'are distinct from but complementary to those . . . for Early Years Professionals' (DfES, 2007), but share the requirement to demonstrate skills in observation and judgement.

The role of the Early Years Professional in the context of new policy is both challenging and multi-dimensional. The creation and implementation of the Early Years Professional Status is central to defining a clear career structure for people entering the Early Years workforce. This structure will be understood and supported by the whole sector and by other children's workforce partners. Moreover, Early Years Professional Status will offer sufficient staff with appropriate skills to deliver the Early Years Foundation Stage, in order to raise and ensure the quality of Early Years provision. The role of the Early Years Professional has a dual purpose: on the one hand, to ensure that polices, legislation, regulatory standards and ethical concerns are met, as well as ensuring that they promote working in partnership. Additionally they have an accountability to deliver the outcomes of EYFS and ECM.

Although the EYPS and the EYFS are positive developments in raising quality in the Early Years, there is some confusion and uncertainty among professionals. Firstly, although it has been suggested that the EYP will have equivalency with qualified teachers, it confers a recognised status and is not a formal qualification. This might lead to lower aspirations among people who are keen to work in the Early Years, but who feel uncertain in terms of having trained to gain a 'status' but not a 'qualification'.

Evidence from research which focused on Early Years practice and pedagogy (Moyles, et al., 2001, Sylva et al., 2001, Siraj Blatchford and Sylva, 2002, Taylor Nelson Sofres and Aubrey, 2002) emphasise that children's cognitive outcomes and learning achievements related positively to adult planned and initiated activities, to shared thinking between adults children and parents and to the level of qualifications of the Early Years workforce. It is now recognised that there is a necessity for well-qualified Early Years practitioners and professionals to have a sound theoretical background following the suggested principles of the EYFS and have a deep understanding of children's development and needs. Children's development and learning is enhanced in environments where professionals are able to observe children's development and to analyse these recordings, as a means of evaluating their activities, and therefore subsequently creating opportunities for furthering children's learning experiences.

The aims of the EYFS are to raise quality, provide for equality of opportunity, offer a framework for partnership working, and to improve safety and security, and considering the child and his or her environment (such as in the family setting), and these objectives are central. The EYP is asked to lead in the delivery all of these aims in a successful way.

There arise two potential problems, the first of which is the increased workload of the EYP. Secondly, the structured curriculum and inspection requirements may become a trap for the Early Years Professional who, in an attempt to meet all the expectations, might ignore or marginalise the developmental and learning needs of the children. The implementation of EYFS in the light of formalised inspection might become a priority, and not the children themselves.

Finally, a wealth of research in the field of the multi agency and inter agency work (Roaf and Lloyd, 1995, Watson, 2002, Puonti, 2004, Warmington, et al., 2004) indicates that crossing professional boundaries in order to work together for effective children's practice is a complex issue. It requires a learning process that takes place within the settings, and also requires the development of a common work culture and an acknowledgment of tension and contradictions. The development of a Common Core of Skills and Knowledge aims to ease these tensions. However, Brown and White (2006) found that in the 'joining up' philosophy of the children's services there are certain limitations for successful integration, such as financial boundaries, cultural differences among professionals, lack of clarity for roles and responsibilities, and a lack of clarity around issues of leadership. They conclude their study by questioning the 'joining up' work ethos with children and caution: 'the complexities of integrated working are unlikely to be overcome to produce its intended benefits unless a clear and sustained focus on the long term-outcomes for clients is maintained' (Brown and White, 2006).

Although there are positive changes and encouraging moves towards raising quality in the Early Years, there is a doubtful and uncertain (as well as confusing) practice context. The Early Years Professional is asked to become both an 'expert' in implementing policy legislation and a 'specialised' educator, in order to deliver the outcomes of the EYFS. The EYP is also asked to become an 'agent of change' in the newly formed integrated services and to communicate with other children's workforce staff on an ongoing basis.

The following sections discuss the role of the EYP in terms of policy context, and also in terms of their role as educator, to highlight how observation can become a tool towards effective practice and partnerships.

The role of the Early Years Professional in the policy context

As mentioned above, an important aspect of the Early Years Professional role is to have a good knowledge and understanding of the policy context, and to be able to understand how this policy context influences practice. In the current policy context the outcomes of the Every Child Matters agenda are the main aims that will dominate your work. However, as changes in the policy occur the Early Years Professional should be able to search for these changes and to keep up to date with all the relevant information. Accessing government websites regularly is important. The EYP is not only responsible for keeping up to date with current legislations and policies, but also has to keep team that he or she works with up to date.

The EYP is responsible for the following.

- Implementing the Early Years Foundation Stage (the statutory duties and the pedagogical aspects of the EYFS).

- Preparing all the documentation for inspections.

- The safety of children.

- Promoting the health of children.

- Promoting effective staff interactions.

- Establishing partnerships with families and with other services.

- Meeting quality standards.

In meeting the Every Child Matters' five outcomes, as has been mentioned in Chapter 2, the Common Assessment Framework is central in identifying any additional needs of children. There is an emphasis on a common process that enables practitioners to undertake an assessment, to which different services and sectors will contribute. For this purpose there is a common form and a common pre-assessment checklist, to help practitioners and professionals to record all the relevant information. The areas covered are as follows.

- Development.

- Health.

- Family and social relationships.

- Self-care skills, independence and learning.

- Safety and protection.

- Emotional warmth and stability.

All these areas are regarded as equally important for a child's well-being. Within this framework the EYP has a key role. In everyday practice the EYP needs to make sure that all children under his or her supervision are meeting the above areas, and to decide whether any additional needs have occurred that need to be addressed. As pointed out in Chapter 2, observations are a useful tool in identifying any needs by collecting pertinent evidence on children's progress. For the effective implementation of the CAF observations are central. Although there are pre-assessment checklists, as well as standardised forms, these alone cannot become independent tools for collecting evidence. As discussed in Chapter 3, when we observe children we try to collect accurate information and specific evidence of what has been seen happening. Consequently, identifying additional needs for the effective implementation of CAF requires the use of a variety of observation techniques, in order to gather information which, after analysis, will lead us to conclude whether the CAF is required or not.

As it can be seen in the context of policy, observations are a key function for effective implementation. Systematic observation can provide the Early Years Professional with valid information in order to put the CAF to effective use.

Moreover, observations can function as a useful communication tool with other professionals. Having collected a wealth of evidence, the required forms can be completed and additional information can also be provided if it is required.

Certain observation skills that the EYP will master can be used in other contexts. Observation skills that the EYP will develop, originally to observe children and the educational programme and its activities, can be transferred to situations where the EYP will be asked to work, either in an inter agency or multi agency environment. Observing other professionals, the language that they use and the ways in which they work, may benefit your own work in terms of reflecting on your own practice. Being able to wait and collect evidence will help you to communicate better, and observing and analysing how other professionals work might become a helpful tool to furthering your understanding when you have to work with others. Different opinions within multi-agency work and inter-agency work is one of the main problems you might have to face within the 'joined up' policy context, and, in practice, when the CAF is implemented. Your observation skills can become your tool, as you will use them to gain an insight into how other sectors operate.

The EYP might use different terminology, and have different priorities and perspectives from those new professional roles that emerge from multi agency and inter agency working. Observing how others function can help you firstly to reflect on your own practice and, secondly, to enable you to get a good understanding for subsequent collaborations with other colleagues.

The role of observations in the context of policy is dualistic. On the one hand, as previously stated, it can facilitate the EYP to implement policies. On the other hand, systematic observation (which includes the analysis of findings, to inform the EYP's own practice) can help to develop a critical approach to policies and can influence practice, policy and legislation.

One of the main responsibilities of the EYP is the delivery of the Early Years Foundation Stage. It is a statutory duty for the EYP to collect evidence, in order to complete the 13 Assessment Scales. These assessments will be used for assessing children's progress, to share information, to promote partnership, and also for inspection purposes. Central to this statutory process is observations as a valid tool, in order to collect all the evidence that you need for the effective completion of these assessment scales. Through observations you can develop a critical approach to them and can voice your opinion to communicate with other Early Years professionals or other services. Bachmann et al. (2006) state: 'clear, positive communication to staff is particularly essential when they are busy with the "day job" and when change has not impacted on them yet. The two-way communication, through, for instance regular learning labs, is crucial to gain staff trust and create and maintain motivation' (p.9).

For example (as was shown in Chapter 3) the assessment scales cannot become mere checklists; further checklists need to be developed, in order to capture precise evidence of the behaviours to be assessed.

PRACTICAL TASK

You work with babies (from 6–12 months) in a day nursery. You want to collect evidence to assess children's physical development. In order to complete the assessment scales on the physical development you have developed the following checklist.

PRACTICAL TASK

Physical development	attempting	yes	no
Has little or no lag when pulled up to sit			
Can lift head and shoulders when lying on front			
Sits with back straight when supported			
Can hold head steady when upright			
When helped standing, takes weight on feet and bounces up and down			
Can roll from front to back			
Can roll from back to front			
Can sit without support			
While sitting can reach forward for a toy without falling over			
Moves around slowly by crawling or bottom shuffling			
Can pull self to standing position			
Can get from a lying down to a sitting position			
Walks around a room holding on to furniture			
Stands alone			
Walks with adult help			
Crawls up stairs			
Walks a few steps alone			
Walks across the room when held by one hand			
Walks pushing large wheeled toys			
Can climb onto a low chair and sit down			

From which items in the assessment checklist of the EYFS (p.48) will you able to collect information?

What items would you have deleted?

What items would you have included?

Observation findings can also be used in your own setting for informal training and staff development purposes. It can enhance and strengthen the links within the team (i.e. team building) and it can become the starting point to discuss critically and reflect on your activities and practice. Team meetings can become effective with observation findings, as you build the discussion upon evidence gathered from your current practice.

> **PRACTICAL TASK**
>
> *Use the example above. Think about how you might start a team meeting to evaluate and modify this checklist.*

The role of the Early Years Professional as educator

The Early Years setting is a context which children can enjoy activities which stimulate them and which help them to develop skills. Early Years settings are learning environments where activities take place in terms of helping children to develop skills, and to explore and make sense of the world. In such environments the practitioners and professionals hold the role of facilitator for children's learning and development. The practitioners and the Early Years Professional should provide an environment where children make progress, taking into consideration children's equality, diversity and inclusion, and enabling children from different cultural backgrounds to interact with one another and share different experiences.

In such an environment the EYP should demonstrate the different facets of the role of educator who facilitates children's development and learning, uses appropriate language, respects values and practices, praises and encourages all children, As the person who is the facilitator of the Early Years learning environment, the EYP has a good understanding of children's development, and of pedagogy, and how these are both linked to their everyday practice. As mentioned in Chapter 1, working in Early Years requires an understanding of the different views of children that form and underpin practice, a good understanding of how children develop, and the different theoretical approaches to this development. This specialised knowledge of the Early Years professional is not isolated to the development of pedagogy through reflection and evaluation of current theories alone.

One of the main common findings of different research projects on pedagogy in Early Years (Moyles, et al., 2001, Sylva et al., 2001, Siraj Blatchford and Sylva, 2002, Taylor Nelson Sofres and Aubrey, 2002) stresses the fact that in Early Years settings where children's learning is most enhanced, the practitioners focus on child-initiated activities and planning, resourcing and assessment are integrated in the daily practice. An important tool for planning and assessment are observations. As mentioned in Chapter 2, observations should be part of the daily routine of the Early Years setting. Everyday observations of children's interactions, their progress within the activities, and the analysis of the observation recordings, all help the EYP to make links between theory and practice, and inevitably to modify their pedagogical principles. For example, in Chapter 2, where Piagetian and Vygotskian ideas were discussed, observations of children's activities were presented to demonstrate how theory is applied in practice.

Moreover, the EYFS emphasise the holistic approach to children's development. In Chapter 5 this view was extended to observations and to children's assessment. To develop a pedagogy that meets the requirements of a holistic approach to children, observations become the means to understand children and parents' diversity, values, and beliefs, and the wider cultural context that children and parents live in and are influenced by. This wider context is not isolated from life in an Early Years setting. Children's experiences in the family context are interlinked with children's experiences in the Early Years setting. In this respect, the role of EYP as an educator has great value. The EYP needs to develop a portfolio of skills and attitudes and to be able to use these skills to develop practice, and to be able to understand the wider context in which children are raised. The EYP needs to listen to children attentively. Powerful tools for this are observations, as they further our understanding and deepen our knowledge of children.

In Chapter 1 conditions for learning were discussed, emphasising children's development, play, children's needs, children's freedom to choose materials and activities, and children's ownership of their learning. As it was explained in Chapter 2, observations offer rich information about children's learning, which enable the EYP to inform future planning and pedagogy. Observations can help as starting points for sharing information among the team. In the role of EYP as educators these observations can become evidence for, and inform, pedagogy and the educational programme and its activities.

PRACTICAL TASK

The following pie chart illustrates the number of children recorded who spent time in different areas of the nursery. Information has been collected over a period of three weeks during play time. Study the diagram and think how you can use this information. How might this inform future planning?

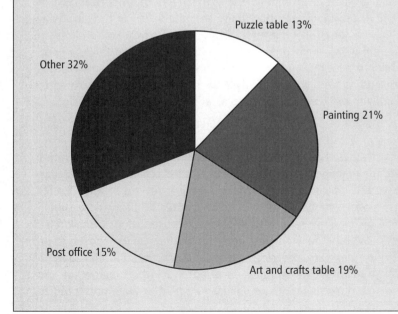

Figure 6.1
Number of children that spent time in play areas in the Early Years setting

Note: Activities accounting for less than 10% (like Home corner, Travel agents, Wood construction, Writing/Drawing table, Dry sand, Wet sand, Water tray, Reading/Quiet carpet, Audio table, Not in an area) of the children's time are not illustrated on the pie chart.

PRACTICAL TASK *continued*

- *Which areas will you enrich?*

- *Which areas might you consider changing?*

- *Which areas might you consider replacing?*

In Chapter 2 it was demonstrated that observations can be used as follows.

- to find out about children as individuals;

- to monitor their progress;

- to inform curriculum planning;

- to enable staff to evaluate the provisions that they make;

- to provide a focus for discussion and improvement;

- to understand Early Years practice better;

- observations are 'woven' into Early Years daily practice.

All of these are important aspects for the everyday practice of the EYP, as it helps to do the following.

- assess children's development and learning, which is statutory in the EYFS as essential for the Early Years programme;

- assess and evaluate the Early Years programme and activities in order to inform practice;

- share this information with children in an appropriate manner for their age;

- share this information with parents;

- share this information with local authorities;

- share this information for the purposes of inspection;

- share information with other practitioners, to exchange ideas and to learn from each other.

The observation process as a tool in Early Years practice assists professionals in developing their specialised knowledge, to gain a deeper understanding of pedagogy and to expand upon pedagogical practices.

The role of the EYP as an educator is not isolated or distinct from the role of the EYP in the context of policy. These are interlinked, and observation skills can become a method for embracing the policy of the educational programme, in order to effectively provide for children.

Alice is 3 years and 11 months old. Her records show that there are some concerns about her social development following her transition from playgroup to nursery, suggesting she has found the change quite difficult to manage. Alice is not integrating with the other children. She shows anxiety when her mother brings her into the nursery. She displays some introverted behaviour and, although she engages with adults, she does not like to make contact or conversations with the other children, nor does she participate in playing with them.

- *How can you plan to help Alice to interact with the other children?*
- *What observation techniques will you use?*
- *How are you going to analyse your findings?*
- *How are you going to share your findings with her parents?*

In your planning consider which behaviours you will observe, and what your aims and objectives will be. In the light of your findings, consider how the team meeting will proceed, and how you are going to investigate whether Alice has any other additional needs.

Think about how the observation process you have designed will assist you to:

- *assess the educational programme, in terms of how it will help Alice to interact with other children;*
- *share information with her parents;*
- *share information with Alice in an appropriate manner.*

CHAPTER SUMMARY

This chapter discussed the role of the Early Years Professional in the two main contexts in which he or she works, in relation to observations in the policy and educational contexts.

As the Early Years Professional Status shares common standards among all people working in the Children's Workforce, there is a need to establish a professional identity with clear roles and responsibilities. The existing policy documentation helps the Early Years professional to understand the legal context of this. The Early Years Foundation Stage offers a framework for the Early Years Professional to deliver the educational programme in relation to developmental learning goals.

Although there is confusion, anxiety and uncertainty, observation skills will be needed for the Early Years Professional irrespective of whether training will change in the future.

In the positive development of creating a workforce for children, the EYP's role is both important and challenging. The training of the EYP is about offering positive attitudes and skills for working with young children. The EYP Standards define national expectations for those who gain EYP Status.

Observations have two roles. Firstly, to help you to develop your practice in the educational context and, secondly, to offer skills to overcome the barriers and the problems of multi-agency work. Observations are a way of developing tools for thinking, whereby systematically collecting evidence and analysing this helps you to communicate ideas at a pedagogical level with the other team members of the Early Years setting. This is necessary in order to meet the goals of the Early Years Foundation Stage, as well as, at a policy level, to communicate ideas with other professionals that you will have to collaborate with to meet the outcomes of Every Child Matters.

FURTHER READING

MacNaughton, G. (ed.) (2003) *Shaping early childhood, learners, curriculum and contexts*, Maidenhead: Open University Press.

Moyles, J. (ed.) (2007) *Early years foundations: meeting the challenge*, Maidenhead: Open University Press.

References

Abbot, L. and Nutbrown, C. (2001) *Experiencing Reggio Emilia: implications for pre-school provision*, Maidenhead: Open University Press.

Aries, P. (1962) *Centuries of childhood. A social history of family life*, Random House.

Athey, C. (1990) *Extending thought in young children*, London: Paul Chapman.

Athey, C. (2007) *Extending thought in young children: a parent-teacher partnership*, 2nd edn, London: Paul Chapman.

Bachmann, M., Husbands, C., Frost, N., Green, J., and Robinson., M. (2006) *Developing multiprofessional teamwork for integrated children's services*, Maidenhead: Open University Press.

Bandura, A. (1971) *Psychological modelling*, New York: Lieber-Atherton.

Bandura, A. (1977) *Social learning theory*, Englewood Cliffs, NJ: Prentice Hall.

Bandura, A. (1986) *Social foundations of thought and action: a social cognitive theory*, Englewood Cliffs, NJ: Prentice Hall.

Bandura, A. (2001) Social cognitive theory: an agentic perspective, *Annual Review of Psychology*, 52, pp. 1–26.

Bandura, A. (1989) Social cognitive theory, in R. Vasta (ed.) (1989) *Annals of child development: theories of child development: revised foundations and current issues*, (vol. 6, pp.1–60)m Greenwich, CT: JAI Press.

Beaty, J. (2005) *Observing for development in young children*, New York: Macmillan.

Benjamin, A.C. (1994) Observations in early childhood classrooms: advice from the field, *Young Children*, 49, 6, pp.14–20.

Benton, M. (1996) The image of childhood: representations of the child in painting and literature, 1700–1900, *Children's Literature in Education*, vol. 27, 1, pp.35–61.

Berk, L.E. (1997) *Child development*, 4th edn, London: Allyn and Bacon.

Brandon, M., Salter, C., Warren, C., Dagely, V., Howe, A., and Black, J. (2006) *Evaluating the common assessment framework and the lead professional guidance and implementation in 2005–6*, Research Brief RB740 April 2006, Annesley, Notts: DfES Publications.

Bronfenbrenner, U. (1977) Towards experimental ecology of human development, *American Psychologist*, 32, pp.513–31.

Bronfenbrenner, U. (1979) *The ecology of human development*, Cambridge, MA: Harvard University Press.

Bronfenbrenner, U. (1989) Ecological systems theory, in R. Vasta (ed.) (1989) *Annals of child development: theories of child development: revised foundations and current issues*, vol. 6, pp.187–251, Greenwich, CT: JAI Press.

Bronfenbrenner, U. (1995) The bioecological model from life course perspective: Reflections of a participant observer, in P. Moen, G.H. Elder and Jr. and K. Luscher (eds) *Examining lives in context*, pp.599–618, Washington: DC: American Psychological Association.

Bronfenbrenner, U. (2005) *Making human beings human*, Thousand Oaks CA: Sage.

Brown, K. and White, K. (2006) Exploring the evidence base for integrated children's services, http://www.scotland.gov.uk/Publications/2006/01/24120649/1 (accessed 25 November 2007).

Bruce, T. (2006) *Early childhood: a guide for students*, London: Sage

Bruce, T. (1997). *Early childhood education*, 2nd edn, London: Hodder and Stroughton.

Bruner, J.S. (1972) *Early childhood education*, London: Hodder and Stoughton

Bruner, J.S. (1977). Introduction, in B. Tizard and D. Harvey (eds) *The biology of play*, London: Spastics International Medical Publications.

Carr M. (1998) *Assessing children's learning in early childhood settings: a development programme for discussion and reflection*, Wellington: New Zealand Council for Educational Research.

Carr, M., (1999) *Learning and Teaching Stories: New Approaches to assessment and Evaluation*, http://www.aare.edu.au/99pap/pod99298.htm (accessed December 2007).

Carr, M. (2001) *Assessment in early childhood settings*, London: Paul Chapman Publishing.

Clark, A. and Moss, P. (2001) *Listening to young children: the Mosaic approach*, London: National Children's Bureau.

CWDC (Children's Workforce Development Council) (2006) *Early years professional national standards*, Leeds: CWDC.

CWDC (2007a) *Early Years Professional National* Standards, Leeds: CWDC.

CWDC (2007b) *Common core of skills and knowledge for the children's workforce,* Leeds: CWDC.

CWDC (2007c) The common assessment framework for children and young people: practititioner's guide, http://www.cwdcouncil.org.uk.pdf (accessed November 2007).

Dahlberg, G. (1991) Empathy and social control. On parent-child relations in context of modern childhood, paper presented at the ISSBD Conference.

David, T. (1993) Educating Children under 5 in the UK, in T. David (ed.), *Educational Provision for our youngest children, European perspective.*, London: Paul Chapman.

DCSF (2008a) *Statutory Framework for the Early Years Foundation Stage*, Nottingham: DCSF.

DCSF (2008b) *Practice Guidance for the Early Years Foundation Stage: Setting the Standards for Learning, Development and Care for Children from Birth to Five*, Nottingham: DCSF.

Department for Education and Skills (2007) *Practice guidance for the early years foundation stage: setting the standards for learning, development, and care for children from birth to five*, London: DfES.

Devereux, J. (2003) Observing children, in J. Devereux and L. Miller (eds) *Working with children in the early years* (2003) (pp.181–202), London: David Fulton Publishers Ltd.

Dewsberry, D.A. (1992) Comparative psychology and ethology: reassessment, *American Psychologist,* 47, pp.208–15.

DfES (1990) *The Rumbold Report*, London: DfES Publications

DfES (2004) *Every child matters: change for children*, Nottingham: DfES Publications.

DfES (2006) Common assessment framework, Available at (http://www.everychildmatters.gov.uk/deliveringservices/caf/ (accessed 28 September 2007).

Dixon, R.A. and Learner, R.M. (1992) A history of systems in developmental psychology, in M.H. Bronstein and M.E. Lamb (eds), *Developmental psychology: an advanced textbook*, 3rd edn, pp.3–58, London: Sage.

Driscoll, V. and Rudge, C. (2005) Channels for listening to young children and parents in A. Clark, A.T. Kjorholt and P. Moss (eds) *Beyond listening*, Bristol: Policy Press.

Drummond, M.J. (1993) *Assessing children's learning*, 1st edn, London: David Fulton.

Drummond, M.J. (1998) Observing children, in S. Smidt (ed.) *The early years: a reader*, London: Routledge.

Drummond, M.J. (2003) *Assessing children's learning*, 2nd edn, London: David Fulton.

Elfer, P. (2005) Observation matters, in L. Abbott and A. Langston (eds) *Birth-to-three matters*, Maidenhead: Open University Press.

Erikson, E.H. (1963) *Childhood and society*, 2nd edn, New York: Norton.

Erikson, E.H. (1982) *The life cycle completed: a review*, New York: Norton.

Eysenck, M.W. (1995) *Principles of cognitive psychology*, London: Royal Holloway University of London.

Faragher, J. and MacNaughton, G. (1998) *Working with young children*, 2nd edn, Melbourne: RMIT Publications.

Fellipini, T., 1995) The role of the pedagogista, an interview with Lella Grandini, in C. Edwards, L. Candini and G. Forman (eds) *The hundred languages of children: the Reggio Emilia approach to early childhood* education, Stamford, CT: Ablex.

Fitzgerald, D. and Kay, J. (2008) *Working together in children's services*, London: Routledge.

Freud, S. (1923) *An outline of psychoanalysis.* London: Hogarth.

Freud, S. (1933) *New introductory lectures in psychoanalysis*, New York: Norton.

Freud, S. (1964) An outline of psychoanalysis, in J. Strachey (ed. and trans) *The standards edition of the complete psychological works of Sigmund Freud* (vol. 23), London: Hogarth Press (original work published 1940).

Glassman, W.E. (2000) *Approaches to psychology,* 3rd edn, Buckingham: Open University Press,

Hamilton, C., Haywood, S., Gibbins, S., McInnes, K., and Williams, J. (2003) *Principles and practice in the foundation stage,* Exeter: Learning Matters.

Harter, S. (1996) The development of self-representation, in W. Damon and N. Eisenberg (eds), *Handbook of child psychology: social, emotional and personality development*, 5th edn, New York: Wiley.

Hartley, D. (1993) *Understanding the nursery school: a sociological analysis*, London: Cassell.

Hendrick, H. (1997) Construction and reconstruction of British childhood: an interpretive survey, 1800 to present, in A. James and A. Prout, 2nd edn, *Constructing and reconstructing childhood: contemporary issues in the sociological study of childhood*, pp.34–63, London: Falmer Press.

HM Government (2004) *The Children Act 2004*, London: HMSO.

HM Government (2006a) *Children's workforce strategy: building a world-class workforce for children, young people and families. The government response to the consultations*, London: DfES.

HM Government (2006b) *The common assessment framework for children and young people: practitioner's guide*, London: The Stationery Office.

Hobart, C, and Frankel, J. (2004) *A practical guide to child observations and assessments*, 3rd edn, Cheltenham: Stanley Thornes.

Hurst, V. (1991) *Planning for early learning*, London: Paul Chapman Publishing.

Katz, L.G.and Chard, S.C. (1989) *Engaging children's minds: the project approach,* Stamford, CT: Ablex.

Klahr, D. (1992). Information processing approaches to cognitive development, in M.H. Bronstein and M.E. Lamb (eds), *Developmental psychology: an advanced textbook*, 3rd edn, pp.3–58, London: Sage.

Lally, M. and Hurst, V. (1992) Assessment in nursery education: a preview of approaches, in G.M. Blenkin and A.V. Kelly (ed.) *Assessment in early childhood education*, pp.69–93, London: Paul Chapman.

Luff, P. (2007) Written observations or walks in the park: documenting children's experiences, in J. Moyles, (ed.) *Early years foundations: meeting the challenge,* Maidenhead: Open University Press.

MacNaughton, G. (ed.) (2003) *Shaping early childhood, learners, curriculum and contexts*, Maidenhead: Open University Press.

Malaguzzi, L. (1993) For an education based on relationships, *Young Children*, November, pp.9–13.

Malaguzzi, L. (1995) History, ideas and basic philosophy: an interview with Lella Gandini, in C. Edwards, L. Gandini and G. Froman (eds) *The hundred languages of children: the Reggio Emilia approach to early Childhood education*, Stamford, CT: Ablex.

Malaguzzi, L. (1996) The hundred languages of children: a narrative of possible (catalogue of the exhibition) Reggio Emilia: Reggio Children.

Miller, L., Hughes, J., Roberts, A., Paterson, L., Staggs, L. (2003) Curricular guidance and frameworks for the early years: UK perspectives, in J. Devereux and L. Miller (eds) *Working with children in the early years*, pp.103–13, London: David Fulton Publishers Ltd.

Mills, J. and Mills, R. (2000) *Childhood Studies: a reader in perspectives of childhood* (ed.), London: RoutledgeFalmer.

Ministry of Education (1996) Te whaariki. He whaariki matauranga mo nga mokopuna O Aoteroa. Early childhood education, Learning Media, http://www.minedu.govt.nz/web/downloadable/dl3567_v1/whariki.pdf (accessed December 2007).

Moore, K. (2001) *Classroom teaching skills*, 5th edn, Oxford: Heinemann.

Moyles, J.R. (1989) *Just playing? The role and status of play in early childhood education*, Milton Keynes: Open University.

Moyles, J. (ed.) (2007) *Early years foundations: meeting the challenge*, Maidenhead: Open University Press

Moyles, J., Adams, S. and Musgrove, A. (2001) *The study of pedagogical effectiveness, a confidential report to the DfES*, Chelmsford: Anglia Polytechnic University.

New Zealand Ministry of Education (1996) *Te whariki. HE whariki matauranga monga-mokopuna o Aotearoa: Early Childhood Curriculum*, Wellington: Learning Media.

Nurse, A. (2008) *The new early years professional*, London: Routledge.

Nutbrown, C. (1999) *Threads of thinking*, London: Paul Chapman

Penn. H. (2005) *Understanding early childhood: issues and controversies*, Maidenhead: Open University Press.

Piaget, J.J. (1929) *The child's conception of the world*, New York: Harcourt Brace.

Piaget, J. (1952) *The origins of intelligence in children*, New York: International Universities.

Piaget, J. (1954) *The construction of reality in the child*, New York: Basic Books.

Piaget, J. (1962) *Play dreams, and imitation in childhood*, New York: W.W. Norton.

Piaget, J. (1965) *Child's conception of language*, London: Routledge and Kegan Paul.

Piaget, J. (1968) *On the development of memory and identity*, Clark University Press: Barre.

Piaget, J. (1969) *The Child's conception of time*, London: Routledge and Kegan Paul.

Pratt, D. (1994) *Curriculum planning: a handbook for professionals*, 2nd edn, Fort Worth: Harcourt Brace.

Puonti, A. (2004) Learning to work together: collaboration between authorities in economic-crime investigation, PhD thesis, University of Helsinki, Department of Education, Centre for Activity Theory and Developmental Work Research, Helsinki: University of Helsinki.

QCA/DfEE (2000) *Curriculum guidance for the foundation stage*, London: QCA.

Riddall-Leech, S. (2005) *How to observe children*, Oxford: Heinemann Educational Publishers.

Rinaldi, C. (1995) The emergent curriculum and social constructivism: an interview with Lella Gandini, in C. Edwards, L. Gandini and G. Froman (eds) *The hundred languages of children: the Reggio Emilia approach to early childhood education*, Stamford, CT: Ablex.

Roaf, C. and Lloyd, C. (1995) *Multi-agency work with young people in difficulty*, Oxford: Oxford Brookes University.

Robinson, M. (2008) *Child development from birth to eight: a journey through the early years*, Maidenhead: Open University Press.

Rodger, R. (2003) *Planning an appropriate curriculum for the under fives*, 2nd edn, London: David Fulton Publishers.

Rousseau, J.J. (1911). *Emile*, trans. B. Foxley, London: Dent.

Salaman, A. and Tutchell, S. (2005) *Planning educational visits for the early years.* London: Sage.

Seefeldt, C. (1990) Assessing young children in C. Seefeldt (ed.) (1990), *Continuing issues in early childhood education*, Upper Saddle River, NJ: Merrill/Prentice Hall.

Shaffer, D. and Kipp, K. (2007) *Developmental psychology: childhood and adolescence*, 7th edn, Belmont: Thomson and Wadsworth.

Simpson, M. and Tunson, J. (1995) *Using observations in small-scale research*, Glasgow: GNP Booth.

Siraj-Blatchford, I. and Sylva, K. (2002) *The effective pedagogy in the early years project, a confidential report to the DfES,* London: London University Institute of Education.

Smidt, S. (2005) *Observing, assessing and planning for children in the early years,* London: Routledge.

Smidt, S. (2007) *A Guide to early years practice*, 3rd edn, London: Routledge.

Sylva, K., Melhuish, E., Sammons, P., and Siraj-Blatchford, I. (2001) The effective provision of pre-school education (EPPE) project. The EPPE symposium at BERA annual conference, University of Leads, September 2001.

Taylor, Nelson Sofres with Aubrey, C. (2002) *The implementation of the foundation stage in reception classes, confidential report to the DfES*, Richmond: Taylor Nelson Sofres.

Tyler, J. (2002) *Te whaariki: the New Zealand curriculum framework*, http://www.worldforumfoundation. org/wf/presentations/index.php?p=2002_tyler (accessed December 2007).

Tyson, P. and Tyson, R.L. (1990) *Psychoanalytical theories of development: an integration*, New Haven, CT: Yale University.

United Nations (1989) Convention on the rights of the child, available at http://www.ohchr.org/english/ law/pdf/crc.pdf (accessed 18 September 2007).

United Nations (1989) *The convention on the rights of the child defense international and the United Nations Children's Fund,* Geneva: United Nations.

Vecci, V. (1995) The role of the atelierista, an interview with Lella Gandini in C. Edwards, L. Candini and G. Forman (eds) *The hundred languages of children: the Reggio Emilia approach to early childhood education*, Stamford, CT: Ablex.

Vygotsky, L. (1986) *Thought and language,* Cambridge, MA: MIT Press.

Vygotsky, L. (1962) *Thought and language*, Cambridge, MA: MIT Press.

Warmington, P., Daniels, H., Edwards, A., Leadbetter, J., Martin, D., Brown, S., and Middleton, D. (2004) Conceptualizing professional learning for multi-agency working and user engagements, paper presented at British Educational Research Association Annual Conference, University of Manchester, 16–18 September 2004.

Watson D., Townsley R. and Abbott D. (2002) Exploring multi-agency working in services to disabled children with complex healthcare needs and their families, *Journal of Clinical Nursing*, 11, pp.367–75.

Willan, J. (2007) Observing children: looking into children's lives, in J. Willan, R. Parker-Ress and J. Savage, (eds) *Early Childhood Studies*, 2nd edn, Exeter: Learning Matters.

Woods, M. and Taylor J. (1998) *Early childhood studies: an holistic introduction,* London: Arnold.

Index